THEOLOGY OF THE BODY

D1440881

Jean-Claude Larchet

Theology
of
the Body

Translated by Michael Donley

ST VLADIMIR'S SEMINARY PRESS
YONKERS, NEW YORK
2016

Library of Congress Cataloging-in-Publication Data

Names: Larchet, Jean-Claude, 1949- author.
Title: Theology of the body / Jean-Claude Larchet ; translated by Michael Donley.
Other titles: Théologie du corps. English
Description: Yonkers, NY : St Vladimir's Seminary Press, 2017.
Identifiers: LCCN 2016059137 (print) | LCCN 2017000329 (ebook) | ISBN
    9780881415605 (alk. paper) | ISBN 9780881415612
Subjects: LCSH: Human body—Religious aspects—Christianity.
Classification: LCC BX1795.B63 L3713 (print) | LCC BX1795.B63 (ebook) | DDC
    233/.5—dc23
LC record available at https://lccn.loc.gov/2016059137

COPYRIGHT © 2017

ST VLADIMIR'S SEMINARY PRESS
575 Scarsdale Road, Yonkers, NY 10707
1-800-204-2665
www.svspress.com

ISBN 978–0–88141–560–5 (paper)
ISBN 978–0–88141–561–2 (electronic)

PRINTED IN THE UNITED STATES OF AMERICA

Table of Contents

Introduction

The human body is a locus of contradictions. This is something we experience first of all in our own body. Its health produces a sense of well-being; its sickness causes us to suffer. Its strength (in any successful physical effort, for example) gives us a feeling of fulfillment; its weakness (in fatigue or any exertion that fails to succeed) makes us aware of its heaviness and limitations. Its beauty is a source of pride, making us effortlessly attractive and significantly facilitating our relationships with others. Its ugliness, on the other hand, gives us complexes, humiliates us, and at times makes our social life more difficult. Its nutritional and reproductive functions enable us to maintain and perpetuate our lives. Yet time, which alters it, and the aches and pains that cause it to deteriorate not only make us experience its irrevocable ageing but, from our youth, cause to hang over us the threat of its corruption and of our death. When it can move freely, it allows us to occupy this or that portion of physical space and to act upon nature, and thereby to experience and enjoy our power and freedom. When its movements are hindered by infirmity or illness, it causes us to experience with sorrow our limitations and finiteness. Most of the time, the body proves to be a faithful servant, subject to the demands of our reason and the control of our will; but it also makes us suffer the burden of its own needs and urges. When we do not submit to them immediately, it imposes on us a struggle that is at times exhausting and which either weakens our will, when we fail, or else strengthens it when we win through, demonstrating at the same time humanity's powers of transcendence.

We sense here, in all its complexity, the ambiguity of the relationship between our soul and our body.

We are aware that we are not purely corporeal beings. We know full well that our body cannot simply be reduced to the sum total of its material components, and that these are structured and animated (that is, literally, endowed with life) by a principle that is superior to them. We also sense that there is in us a transcendent power by means of which we can begin to act or stop, start to do something or not, give free reign to such and such a movement of the body or hold it in check, satisfy a certain inclination or refuse to do so, guide the body in this direction or that. To a large extent we feel able to control and master our body. Despite its demands, we feel we are independent of it. Sensing, then, that we cannot simply be reduced to our physical bodies, we feel instinctively that, after the body's death, we shall continue to exist. In moments of concentration, contemplation, or rapture—before the beauty of creation or art, for example, or during prayer—we may even go so far as to forget about our body altogether. Other experiences can make us perceive it to be something extraneous and distant, as if not really an essential aspect of our self but as something added on, like a garment whose removal would not prevent us from remaining fundamentally what we are, or like a tool that might extend our hand, but without really belonging to it.

And yet, we feel that we are not pure spirits either. As noted, the body constantly makes us aware of its heaviness, its weaknesses, its limitations, and consequently those of our entire being. What we have eaten or drunk, the sleep we have had too much or too little of—these simple things affect not just our psychological state but our spiritual state as well. An important part of the body's functions lies outside our control. Moreover, it seeks to impose on us its needs, its inclinations, and its whims. It does so overwhelmingly, as suggested above, when it is a question of hunger, thirst, pain, sorrow, or the desire for sleep—all of which are able to paralyze many of the functions of our soul.

The body and the soul derive pleasure or pain by turns from that which differentiates them as much as from their intimate union.

Sometimes their co-existence expresses itself as a fruitful collaboration, sometimes as an intolerable cohabitation. Their common life fluctuates between being a case of troublesome tension or a blissful feeling of unity and harmony.

It is when faced with other people that we become aware of all the body's advantages and inconveniences. To begin with, it is through our body that we reach out to others and make contact with them—by exchanging glances, smiling at them, holding their hand, and so on. And it is through our body that others meet us and gain a first impression of our personality, our character, or our mood at the time. Our body reveals to them and yet at the same hides from them just who we are. What they perceive in the first place is the objective dimension of our self. In other words, they encounter us as an object before knowing us as a subject.[1] They perceive us on the basis of external appearances before getting to know us in the intimate and profound reality of our inner life. The view and opinion they form about us on the basis of these appearances may embarrass and upset us, to the point of making us feel we have lost our transcendence and freedom.[2] But they can also arouse in us interest and hope, being seen as a call to mutual discovery and dialogue, making us experience the importance we have for others, and giving us or giving us back our sense of personal worth.

It is by our body's physical appearance—particularly our face, its most eloquent feature, and even more so our expression, which is the very center of the face[3]—it is by the body's gestures and attitudes that, whether we mean to or not, we attract other people, charm them, inspire their sympathy, awaken love in them; or, on the contrary, provoke aversion, suspicion, or antipathy. But we are also able to make use of our body so as to contribute to shaping or

[1]See J. P. Sartre, *Being and Nothingness*, Hazel E. Barnes, trans. (New York: Philosophical Library Inc., 1956), Part Three, chapters 1 and 2.

[2]Ibid.

[3]See Olivier Clément, *Le Visage intérieur* (Paris: Éditions Stock, 1978), 13–25. E. Lévinas, *Totality and Infinity: An Essay on Exteriority*, A. Lingis, trans. (Pittsburgh, PA: Duquesne University Press, 1969), 197ff. Exteriority and the Face.

altering the image people have of us—whether that image be more or less accurate, more or less false—or even so as to construct in their eyes, and our own, the image we would like them to have.[4] We can let them know in part who we are, by endeavoring to make that which our body expresses coincide with what we feel inwardly. But we can also lie to them about ourselves. Thus, by controlling our bodily expressions, we are able to hide our inner state. All the same, through the emotions it feels or as a result of subconsciously deliberate slips, our body may still convey to others that which we would like to hide.

By its unique physical form, my body instantly reveals to other persons their difference from me and mine from them. This difference, this otherness might seem to be an obstacle to communion and mutual understanding; but it also proves to be that which makes discovery and exchange possible. At the same time that our bodies reveal our differences—and even our radical personal otherness— they also reveal what we have in common as members of a single human nature. For example, it is by similar signs that our bodies convey feelings of pleasure or pain, and other such emotions.

Christianity has, from its beginnings, been fully aware of these ambiguities, contradictions, and tensions. Throughout its development, it has never ceased to experience them in its midst. Indeed, in many respects Christian anthropology and spirituality bear witness to a desire to understand and resolve them. It is this that we would like to demonstrate in the following pages, basing ourselves in particular on the foundational teaching of Scripture and the Fathers. In our opinion, this teaching retains a contemporary relevance that can help give meaning to our body at a time and in a culture that, in this respect, has largely lost its bearings.

It must be admitted that, by allowing distorted forms of asceticism and moralism to develop in its midst, Western Christianity bears a heavy responsibility for the depreciation and even rejection

---

[4]See Pascal, *Pensées*, J. M. Cohen, trans. (Harmondsworth: Penguin Classics, 1961), 68–70, 72.

of the body that our culture has known in the past and, as a consequence, for the backlash to which this has given rise. The effects of this can be seen today in the glorification of the body as an object and instrument of pleasure—neglect of the body having been replaced by neglect of the soul, as if by a swing of the pendulum.

The fact remains that original, authentic Christianity is, by its very nature, the one religion that values the body most of all. This is seen in its doctrine of creation, whereby the body too is deemed to be made in the image of God. Similarly, Christianity's portrayal of future life is one in which the body is also called to participate. Indeed, it is seen in its conception of the human person as composed inextricably of soul and body, and who thus does not simply *have* a body but in part *is* a body, marked by all its spiritual qualities. Without question, such exceptional value and significance accorded the body is linked to the very basis of Christianity—namely, the incarnation. It is a consequence of the fact that the Son of God became man, assuming not simply a human soul but a human body; that in this body he experienced what we experience; that in his person he delivered it from its weaknesses and ills, making it incorruptible, granting it eternal life; and that he gave it as food to his disciples and believers, making them partakers of his divinity, and of all the associated blessings.

CHAPTER ONE

The Body in Its Original State

1. *The Body's Relationship to the Soul and the Spirit.*

In the biblical account of creation, one is struck by the fact that it is the human body that God creates first: "Then God formed man *out of dust from the ground*, and breathed in his face the breath of life; and man became a living soul" (Gen 2.7). The dust designates the body, the breath of life the soul. Here, Scripture contradicts in advance those philosophical or religious schools of thought—such as Platonism, Gnosticism, Neoplatonism, or Origenism—that see the body as a secondary, subsequent entity, associated with a degradation of reality, or a fall of the soul resulting from a transgression committed in a state that was originally incorporeal.[1] This primacy granted the body by the Creator himself is part of the rationale that lies behind biblical anthropology's acknowledgement of its pre-eminent value—something that Christianity has made its own.

The assertion that the first human being was "formed out of dust from the ground" might be thought to reflect a conception of the body that is pejorative; yet biblical expositors have drawn from it quite different lessons. It shows, for example, the power of God in

[1]Platonism considers the body (*sōma*) to be a tomb (*sēma*) into which the soul, celestial by nature, has fallen and become imprisoned. As for Gnosticism—whose various forms agree on this point—the body is a material creation linked to the Aeons (spirits), imprisoning them in proportion to their distance from the divine source from which they emanate. In the Neoplatonism associated with Plotinus, the body belongs to the material world, which corresponds to the inferior stage in the process of divine emanation, the one following on from the degradation of the One into the Intellect and then the Soul. The Origenist school of thought sees in the body a material creation into which the soul fell and became imprisoned as a result of a transgression committed in the celestial world where, united to the other souls, it had led a divine life.

13

being able to fashion so complex a being from practically nothing. It shows, too, that humans contain within themselves the various basic elements from which everything else in the universe is formed, God having in this way made us to be microcosms who recapitulate and unify the whole of creation, whose most perfect beings we are.[2] As for "dust," some see this as referring to the purest part of the earth, a soil as yet untilled and virgin.[3]

It is also striking that in the same verse from Genesis man is already recognizably present in his body even before his soul has been added: "Then God formed *man* out of dust from the ground." Thus, from the very beginning, the body is regarded as being human, as being an essential part of the human being, as a reality that is already "man." However, this does not mean that it is something that can suffice or subsist by itself. As the biblical account also specifies, God breathed into the body "the breath of life," that is, a soul. It was only at that moment that man was really formed and became a living being.

According to Christian anthropology, this soul is made up of two components: the soul proper (*psychē, anima*), and the spirit (*nous, spiritus*).

The soul proper comprises three "parts" that the Fathers, following Aristotle, sometimes portray as three different souls—the better to show that, in addition to the specifically human dimension, human beings are also composed of that which characterizes the vegetable and animal kingdoms.[4] But here it is more accurately a question of the three major functions or "powers" of the human soul, which is in itself single and undivided.[5]

[2]See Gregory of Nyssa, *On the Soul and the Resurrection* 12. Maximus the Confessor, *Ambigua* 41, 43; *Mystagogia* 7. John of Damascus, *An Exact Exposition of the Orthodox Faith* 2.12. Gregory Palamas, *Homily* 53.

[3]See Philo of Alexandria, *On the Creation* 47. Irenaeus of Lyons, *Against the Heresies* 2.21.10; *On the Apostolic Preaching* 2.

[4]See Gregory of Nyssa, *On the Making of Man* 8, 29. Nemesius of Emesa, *On the Nature of Man* 15. Maximus the Confessor, *Third Century on Love* 32. John of Damascus, *An Exact Exposition* 2.12.16. Nicetas Stethatos, *On the Soul* 31–32.

[5]See Gregory of Nyssa, *On the Making of Man* 14; *On the Soul and the Resurrection* 42–43.

At the most elementary level is the vegetative or vital power common to all living things, whether human, animal, or vegetable. It is this that is the source of life in any organism and that, in particular, assures the functioning of the vital organs. Its other main function is the regulating of nutrition, growth, and generation.

At the second level is the animal power, common to humans and animals. In addition to the capacity of sensation and perception, it comprises two main faculties or powers: the incensive power, from which spring all forms of aggressiveness (including, in the case of human beings, the combative aspect of the will); and the appetitive power, the source of emotions, desires, and affectivity.[6] Linked to it is the imagination in its elementary form, i.e., the reproductive imagination.[7]

At the third level is the rational power, which is specific to humans and which constitutes the principal characteristic of our nature, distinguishing us from all other created beings. It is characterized in the first place by the reason and all the faculties associated with it: reflexive consciousness; abstract thought; a linguistic function (humans alone being endowed with speech precisely because we are endowed with reason); memory and imagination in their higher forms, the one enabling us to retain and recall abstract knowledge, the other to invent and create. Secondly, it is characterized by its capacity of self-determination, which is the source of our freedom and to which are connected free will (the faculty of choice) and the higher dimension of the will, which enables the choices made to be carried out.

The spirit (or intellect) is generally portrayed by the Fathers as the highest part of the soul but also at times—the more strongly to emphasize its transcendence—as a distinct faculty, superior to the soul.[8] It is the spirit that is the primary source of the consciousness

[6]This idea, which can already be found in Plato, was taken up again by Freud in his distinction between Eros and Thanatos—the first term representing all those drives that relate to desire, the second those relating to aggression, of which the death wish is the most extreme.

[7]To be distinguished from the creative imagination, which can form new images.

[8]Thus one comes across the trichotomy body-soul-spirit rather than the

(both reflexive and moral), of the intelligence, and also of the capacity for self-determination, which makes human beings capable of self-control, independence, and freedom.[9] More specifically, the spirit enables us to have intuitive, intellectual knowledge of a kind superior to rational knowledge and also, most importantly, to have direct knowledge—or knowledge by revelation—of spiritual realities. In other words, it constitutes the contemplative faculty (*theōrētikē*). For the Fathers, it is essentially that by which man is linked to God objectively and definitively from the first moment of his creation. In fact, the spirit is par excellence the image of God in man. This image may be masked or sullied by sin, but not destroyed. For it is the indelible hallmark of the deepest part of our being, of our true nature whose essential constituent principle (or *logos*) cannot be altered.

According to the Fathers, Adam was created as an inseparable union of soul and body, characterized by both of them together, neither by itself being sufficient to define him as such. As St Irenaeus puts it, "that flesh which has been molded is not a perfect man in itself, but the body of a man, and part of a man. Neither is the soul itself, considered apart by itself, the man; but it is the soul of a man, and part of a man."[10] In asserting that the human being is a soul and at the same time a body, the Fathers oppose every form of materialism or naturalism that would reduce us to being thought of as nothing but physical, biological entities; that would deny the existence of the soul or limit it to being a mere epiphenomenon of the body, derived from it and determined by it; and that see in the body alone the principle of every action that we undertake and every state that we experience.

---

dichotomy body-soul. On this question see in particular A. J. Festugière, "La division corps-âme-esprit de 1 Thess 5.23 et la philosophie grecque" in his *L'Idéal religieux des Grecs et l'Évangile* (Paris: Librairie Lecoffre, 1932), 196–220.

[9]See Athanasius of Alexandria, *Against the Heathen* 32. Gregory of Nyssa, *On the Soul and the Resurrection* 101. Nemesius of Emesa, *On the Nature of Man* 3, 22. John of Damascus, *An Exact Exposition* 2.12.

[10]Irenaeus, *Against the Heresies* 5.6.1. See Justin Martyr, *On the Resurrection*.

In insisting correlatively that the body is an integral part of our very being—acknowledging that its dignity is equal to that of the soul, and refusing to ascribe to it a different origin and destiny—the Fathers also refute those spiritualistic conceptions according to which the body is on the one hand merely an avatar of the soul—evidence of its fall, a source of impurity, a tomb that by chance imprisoned it,[11] a non-essential element added on—and, on the other hand, that the soul by itself constitutes the essence of a human being and will only reveal and fulfill itself by becoming detached from the body through a progressive negation of the latter.

We are, then, at once both soul and body, a composite of two substances. The Fathers never cease repeating that the human being is double, compound by nature, and that its essence consists of both constituents taken as a whole.[12]

This affirmation of a double constitution, of the co-existence of these two substances and yet their clear distinction does not, however, reflect a conception that is dualist; for the Fathers simultaneously stress the human composite's unity.[13] We are one in two substances. This is all the more the case since soul and body have a simultaneous origin in a single creative act.[14] This communion between the two—produced by God when he created Adam in the beginning—is reproduced at the conception of each new person, "one element [not being placed before] the other, neither the soul before the body, nor the contrary."[15] Even death does not abolish the unity of the human composite. It separates body and soul in a relative sense only, since in death neither soul nor body exist in isolation

[11]See Plato, *Gorgias* 493a; *Cratylus* 400c.

[12]See Irenaeus of Lyons, *Against the Heresies* 2.15.3; *On the Apostolic Preaching* 2. Athenagoras, *On the Resurrection of the Dead* 18, 25. Cyril of Jerusalem, *Catechetical Lectures* 4.18. Gregory of Nyssa, *Easter Sermons* 3. John Chrysostom, *Homilies on Genesis* 14.5. Gregory Palamas, *Prosopopoeia*.

[13]See Gregory of Nyssa, *On the Making of Man* 29.

[14]See Gregory of Nyssa, *Ibid.* 28–29. Nicetas Stethatos, *On the Soul* 14, 26; *Letters*, 4.9.

[15]See Gregory of Nyssa, *On the Making of Man* 29.1. Maximus the Confessor, *Letters* 12, 13; *Ambigua* 42.

but are always the soul and body not simply of a human being, but of a particular human being, considered as a whole and of whom they remain the "parts."[16]

This brief outline shows that the Fathers constantly seek to protect a balanced understanding of the human being's constitution—the two substances that make it up being distinguished without being separated, united without being confused.[17] Thus it is not possible fully to envisage the one without the other, to think of a human being in terms of one independently of the other, although each retains its own nature and to some extent its own destiny.[18]

The interweaving of soul and body implies that in every human activity they act simultaneously and experience the same affections, the same emotions, the same passions.[19] "On account of its bond with the body, the soul seems both to be subject to its influence and to impress upon it its own."[20] In this way any movement of the soul is accompanied by a movement of the body, and vice versa.[21] Every act, movement, or state of the human being is an act, movement, or state of soul and body simultaneously.

This is because, in the human composite, no element can act without the other being involved. Without the soul, the body can accomplish nothing.[22] Likewise the soul without the body, though for different reasons: the body needs the soul in order to live and move,[23] whereas the soul needs the body in order to reveal itself,

[16]See Maximus the Confessor, *Ambigua* 42.

[17]See Symeon the New Theologian, *The Practical and Theological Chapters* 2.23. Nemesius of Emesa, *On the Nature of Man* 3.

[18]See John of Damascus, *An Exact Exposition* 3.16. Isaac the Syrian, *Ascetical Homilies* 83 [numbering follows the Greek and French editions, see p. 104—*Ed.*].

[19]See Gregory of Nyssa, *Easter Sermons* 3. Maximus the Confessor, *Letters* 12; *Centuries on Love* 2.57. John of Damascus, *An Exact Exposition* 2.12. Gregory Palamas, *The Triads* 2.2.12.

[20]Nemesius of Emesa, *On the Nature of Man* 3.

[21]See Evagrius Ponticus, *On Prayer* 63, 68. Isaac the Syrian, *Ascetical Homilies* 83. Maximus the Confessor, *Questions and Doubts* 149; *Centuries on Love* 2.85, 92.

[22]See Nicetas Stethatos, *On the Soul* 56.

[23]See Nemesius of Emesa, *On the Nature of Man* 2. Nicetas Stethatos, *On the Soul* 56.

to express itself, and to act on the external world.[24] For the body is the servant, the vehicle or instrument of the soul,[25] essential to the exercise of its functions of relating to the world and manifesting its faculties in the conditions of its earthly existence. In this setting, all of the soul's activities, insofar as they reveal themselves, can only exist through the body.[26] Moreover, they remain unexpressed if the necessary bodily organs are unable to function properly. Such is the case with some illnesses that prevent these organs from expressing certain of the soul's capacities, something for which they had naturally been ordered. It is also the case with the embryo, in which they are not yet developed, as is clearly explained by St Gregory of Nyssa:

> Even if [the soul] is not visibly recognized by any manifesta-
> tions of activity, it none the less is there; for even the form of
> the future man is there potentially, but is concealed because it
> is not possible that it should be made visible before the neces-
> sary sequence of events allows it; so also the soul is there, even
> though it is not visible, and will be manifested by means of its
> own proper and natural operation, as it advances concurrently
> with the bodily growth; . . . the energies of the soul also grow
> with the subject in a manner similar to the formation and per-
> fection of the body.[27]

Thus a human being is recognizably such from the beginning of its existence, soul and body being from the outset united in the person who already exists. Whereas the body exists only in an embryonic state, the soul and the spirit are fully present from the start, even

[24]See Gregory of Nyssa, *On the Making of Man* 15.

[25]See John Chrysostom, *Homilies on Genesis* 14.5. Nemesius of Emesa, *On the Nature of Man* 2. John of Damascus, *An Exact Exposition* 2.12. Nicetas Stethatos, *On the Soul* 62.

[26]One can even say that the soul's general state leaves its mark on the body, particularly the face. See John Cassian, *Conferences* 7.1. John Climacus, *The Ladder of Divine Ascent* Step 30.17, Colm Luibheid and Norman Russell, trans. (Mahwah, NJ: Paulist Press, 1982), 287–88. As the author of Ecclesiasticus had already observed, "The heart of a man changes the expression on his face/ Either for good or for evil" (Sir 13.24).

[27]Gregory of Nyssa, *On the Making of Man* 29.4.6.

though the degree to which they are able to manifest themselves is commensurate with that of the body's development. For this reason the Greek Fathers[28]—who do not share the opinion of Aristotle (taken up again in the Middle Ages by Thomas Aquinas) that the specifically human, rational soul is infused into the body several months after it has come into being—consider abortion to be a crime, even if carried out in the first weeks of the embryo's existence.[29]

The above considerations, which emphasize the close union of soul and body, should not cause us to forget that the soul is different in nature from the body, being incorporeal[30] and retaining supremacy over it.[31] It is the soul that gives life to the body;[32] it is to the soul that the body owes its organization; it is the soul that governs the body's activity and maintains its unity.[33] Indeed, the interlinking of soul and body is itself due to the soul, which permeates the latter entirely,[34] as light permeates the air.

The same is true of the spirit: it is not exterior to the body[35] but, like the soul, is united to it—not partially but in its entirety—and permeates it totally,[36] just as it permeates the soul.[37]

[28]See especially Gregory of Nyssa, *On the Making of Man* 29. Maximus the Confessor, *Ambigua* 42.

[29]For a more detailed examination of this matter, see our *Pour une éthique de la procréation: Éléments d'anthropologie patristique* (Paris: Éditions du Cerf, 1998), 76–85.

[30]See Maximus the Confessor, *Letters* 6. Nemesius of Emesa, *On the Nature of Man* 3.

[31]See, among others, Athanasius of Alexandria, *Against the Heathen* 31, 32. Maximus the Confessor, *Centuries on Love* 1.7.

[32]See Gregory of Nyssa, *On the Soul and the Resurrection* 14, 28–29.

[33]See Maximus the Confessor, *Ambigua* 7, 42. John of Damascus, *An Exact Exposition* 2.12. Nicetas Stethatos, *On the Soul* 24. Gregory Palamas, *Topics of Natural and Philosophical Science and on the Moral and Ascetic Life* 3, 30.

[34]See Nemesius of Emesa, *On the Nature of Man* 3. Macarius of Egypt, *Homilies* as paraphrased by Symeon Metaphrastis 67. Athanasius of Alexandria, *Against the Heathen* 32. Gregory of Nyssa, *On the Soul and the Resurrection* 29, 32. Maximus the Confessor, *Ambigua* 7.

[35]See Athanasius of Alexandria, *Against the Heathen* 32. Gregory of Nyssa, *On the Making of Man* 15.

[36]See Gregory of Nyssa, *On the Making of Man* 12, 14, 15.

[37]Ibid. 14.

By this union the body, together with the soul, acquires the possibility of partaking fully in the spiritual life. In fact, the spirit has the power to subjugate all the other elements of the human composite, the power to conform them to itself and to spiritualize them by communicating, even to the most intimate depths of their being, the divine energies which, by reason of its nature, it is the most apt and the first to receive. Thus through its mediation we—our soul but also our body—can be united with God and become partakers of divine life with our whole being.

2. *The Body, Created in the Image of God.*

The importance and value accorded the body by Christianity stems not just from the fact that it is linked to the soul and the spirit, sharing after its own fashion in man's spiritual life, but also from the fact that, according to the account in Genesis, it was the total man who was created in the image of God: "Then God said, 'Let us make man in our image, according to our likeness.' . . . So God made man; in the image of God he made him" (Gen 1.26–27). The majority of the Fathers emphasize that essentially it is our spirit that was created in God's image, not simply because the spirit is endowed with intelligence, is capable of self-determination, and enjoys freedom (these being our highest faculties and the ones that God possesses in pre-eminent fashion), but also because the spirit possesses divine qualities such as immateriality, incorruptibility, immortality, and impassibility. Many of the Fathers hesitate to consider the body as also being constituted in the image of God, but this seems to be above all for pedagogical reasons: they wish to avoid our concluding that God himself has a body or is in some sense material. Nevertheless, some Fathers do consider that the body, too, was made in the image of God[38]—an interpretation, moreover, which adheres to the account in Genesis, which in this respect makes no separation

---

[38]See Irenaeus of Lyons, *Against the Heresies* 5.6.1–2; 5.16.1; *On the Apostolic Preaching* 2. John Chrysostom, *Homilies on Genesis* 8.3. Gregory Palamas, *Prosopopoeia.* This idea is found in most of the Syrian exegetes.

between soul and body but embraces the human being as a whole. Certain Fathers justify this point of view by emphasizing that the body is in a sense enveloped and encompassed by the spirit, which entirely permeates it.[39] Others do so having in mind the body's beauty in its original state—a visible reflection of God's own beauty. Yet others argue, more profoundly, that man was created in the image of Christ, the incarnate Word,[40] God having foreseen from all eternity the incarnation of the Son.

3. *The Body, a Dimension of the Person.*

The body is not simply an element belonging to human nature; it is also a dimension of the human person.

If, as humans, we all have the same nature—whose specific characteristics distinguish us from the nature of beings belonging to other genera and species—we are at the same time distinct, diverse persons. According to our nature we are all alike; as persons, we are all different, each unique. My nature is *what* I am; my person is *who* I am. As persons we each assume the common nature in a singular, unique manner. In other words, we are each human in a fashion unique to ourselves. Thus, according to our nature, we are all endowed with reason, memory, and imagination; we all have affections (pleasure or pain), emotions, and feelings; we all have a will and can exercise freedom of choice. However, as persons we are endowed with this reason, this memory, and this imagination in differing degrees, and we make of them different uses. As for pleasure and pain, we each feel them in our own way; we are moved in our own way; we love in a manner unique to ourselves; we use our freedom in a singular fashion; we pursue our own aims, make our own choices, and seek to execute them with varying degrees of determination.

Personhood is not the same thing as character, which merely corresponds to a particularization of human nature on the psychological

[39]See Gregory of Nyssa, *On the Making of Man* 12.
[40]See Irenaeus of Lyons, *Against the Heresies* 4.33.4; 5.16.1–2. Nicholas Cabasilas, *The Life in Christ* 6.91–92. In English 6.12, in *The Life in Christ,* C.J. deCantazaro, trans. (Crestwood, NY: St Vladimir's Seminary Press, 1982), 191.

level. It is possible to distinguish various types of character and many different people may have the same character, but personhood is absolutely unique.

A person is also to be distinguished from an individual, for individuality is simply a biological and social category. On the social level, individuals are distinct but interchangeable within the context of the social category to which they belong. On the biological level, individuals are distinct and different—each is even unique—but only as concerns purely physical characteristics. Thus the concept of individuality may be applied not just to man, but to animals and plants. The term "person," on the other hand, can only be used of spiritual beings—human beings, angels, the divine persons—who are endowed with intelligence, will, and freedom, albeit in different degrees. Thus the Fathers have often seen the spirit—which is the source of these attributes—as being the "seat" of the person. This concept of "person" connotes both transcendence and worth. On the one hand, persons are more than that which defines their nature on the biological and social level; for, as persons, we each have the capacity constantly to surpass ourselves as well as the possibility of being raised by divine grace to a spiritual state wherein our nature's mode of existence is transcended. On the other hand, persons, as such, possess an absolute value which renders them totally unique and irreplaceable.

Needless to say, it is a value that applies to our entire being; for our soul and body belong to our person, which they express and manifest each in their own way. Thus, since the body is a dimension of the person, it too possesses specific characteristics, a unique character, and likewise a value that is absolute. This is the basis for the respect we owe to our own body as well as to that of every other person. It also confers on the body a spiritual dimension and value, which means that it can no longer be seen as a purely physical substance nor be separated from the man or woman whose body it is. By the same token, the body shares in the spiritual development of the person as a whole.

In the eyes of the Fathers, then, the body is an integral part of the person, participating in its spiritual value from the moment of conception and beyond its life on earth. This, together with the fact that soul and body are inseparable elements of the human composite, is the basis for asserting that it is possible for a person to reacquire—albeit according to another mode of existence—the same body that had been provisionally separated from the soul by death. It also justifies Christianity's rejection of abortion, as well as the doctrine of metempsychosis or reincarnation.[41] Indeed, abortion is considered by the Fathers to be an attack on the life of an actual person since, as seen, they consider the person to be inseparably present from the moment of conception—we humans not being able to exist as such other than as persons. As for the doctrine of metempsychosis or reincarnation—widespread in Antiquity and found again today not only in certain Far Eastern religions but in various more or less fanciful theories of New Age thinking—it is incompatible with the Christian conception of personal identity. We cannot be different persons successively nor have different identities at different times. It is a doctrine that runs counter to Christianity's understanding of the body as belonging to our person and thus as having an inseparable link with our soul and our spirit.[42] Thus one cannot have several bodies, one after the other. The spiritual body which, after the general resurrection, will replace the carnal body in the kingdom of heaven (cf. 1 Cor 15.35–53) will admittedly be different as regards condition and mode of existence, but not as regards personal identity. According to the Christian faith, it is our own present body that will rise again.

It is in and through a human being's person that the body is indissolubly united with the soul and the spirit. This is also what explains the body's uniqueness, as well as its spiritual significance and value. Furthermore, it is this—the fact that the body is always considered, on the one hand, as being inseparable from the other two constituent elements of the human being and, on the other, as being

[41]See Maximus the Confessor, *Ambigua* 42.
[42]See Gregory of Nyssa, *On the Soul and the Resurrection* 59–62, 68.

that of a person—that prevents it from being considered or treated as a separate entity or as something impersonal.

In this regard, the Christian conception of the body is to be distinguished from the understanding which is generally that of modern medicine, limited as it is to the framework of the natural sciences. Many doctors today no longer treat persons, but bodies or even organs. As a result, many patients suffer from being thought of and treated as objects—cut off from one dimension of their being, fragmented and at the same time degraded to the level of general "cases," reduced by means of analytical instruments to being mere strings of numbers. Of course, a Christian view of medicine cannot reject scientific training, for it offers an assurance of rigor and protects against those irrational, wayward trends that nowadays are increasing in number by way of reaction. However, it is a question not simply of bringing to patients and their therapy a little something extra,[43] but of taking into consideration the totality of what we understand a human being to be—that is, not merely a body but also a soul and a spirit which are connected with this body and which, whether positively or negatively, have an effect on it. On the other hand, it is also a question of taking into consideration the patients' reality as persons, which means that each case is singular, each person's constitution, way of life, and destiny being unique.[44]

This Christian conception is opposed just as radically to those other portrayals of the body that our society has developed, in which it is both objectified and thoroughly fragmented.

The advertisements that are everywhere in our streets and on our television screens cunningly foist on us a representation of the body in which it is deprived of any spiritual or personal dimension

---

[43]In the original, Larchet uses here the phrase "un supplément d'âme." This colloquial idiom can also be rendered as "an additional sensitivity, something special or extra, a personal touch." However, given its literal meaning and the fact that it is in inverted commas, it seems clear that in choosing it for this particular context he is enjoying an untranslatable play on words.—*Trans.*

[44]For a more in-depth treatment of this topic, see our *Le Chrétien devant la maladie, la souffrance et la mort* (Paris: Éditions du Cerf, 2002). In particular, see ch. 6, "Pour une approche chrétienne du malade," 75–94.

at all, and is instead reduced to being nothing more than its physical appearance. In a world left at the mercy of commercial forces, the body—especially the naked body—has become simply a means of arousing covetousness, by displacement onto the objects with which it is associated and from which it seems to benefit, being entirely placed at the service of the products whose sales it is being used to promote.

In the violence that we see increasing day by day in modern society, and that literature and above all the cinema delight in portraying in its most extreme forms, a view of the body is presented in which—considered independently of the soul and spirit to which it is linked, as well as of the person to which it belongs—it no longer commands respect, but is treated as a worthless object that can be used as one pleases and whose very life no longer seems to be an essential, inviolable attribute.

This objectification and deconstruction reaches a peak in the pornography that is propagated in modern civilization by the marketing of images, with its exploitation of the crudest of human passions. Casual partners are drearily brought together, each ignorant of the other's personality, history, and even identity. Between the two no spiritual relationship exists, of course; not even an affective one. Contact between them is exclusively physical. Their bodies—reduced to the level of mere objects and become nothing but tools at the service of their instincts and fantasies—engage in performances in which the sexual organs, dissociated from the rest of the body, are dedicated to functions which have lost even their biological dimension, behaving like machines and peddling the illusion of intense, prolonged pleasure.

In such a world, the portrayal of the body afforded by Christian anthropology (and the ethics that stem from it) proves to be genuinely salutary. For if, as that anthropology teaches, any attack on the body is an attack on the very person, conversely any respect shown the body is evidence of respect for the person. Such respect is not only the necessary foundation for nobler sentiments such as charity but is indispensable in establishing with others—and even oneself—relationships which are not just harmonious but fully and genuinely human.

4. *The Body, Created for the Divine Likeness.*

God made man not only in his image but also according to his likeness: "Let us make man in our image, according to our likeness" (Gen 1.26). Most of the Fathers distinguish between these two notions, giving them different meanings. The image is actual, already realized; the likeness, on the other hand, is potential or virtual, something still to be accomplished. Whereas the image relates to our nature and is independent of our will—which is why it remains a permanent characteristic of every human being—the likeness relates to our person and depends on our choices, on the inclination of our will, on our way of life as shown in our moods, our inner states, and our actions. Yet the two concepts are not unrelated. On the one hand, it is the image that makes us aim at achieving this likeness and which, moreover, contains the necessary powers and means that it is our responsibility to make use of in attaining it. On the other hand, the realization of the likeness corresponds to an actualization of the image's potential. In other words, to strive for the likeness enables us to accomplish, in our own person, our nature as humans, to flourish, and to realize ourselves fully.

For the Fathers, it is by means of the virtues that we can become like God,[45] and it is in this likeness to God, acquired by a collaboration between free will and the grace given us that we can ultimately become a partaker of divine life—a participation to which we are both destined by our nature and called by personal vocation.

A life lived virtuously involves both soul and body, even if it is true that some virtues are more of the soul (such as humility) and others more of the body (such as temperance). For we have seen that we are inextricably both soul and body, that our spirit entirely permeates and envelopes both, that our body always takes part, to a

[45]See John of Damascus, *An Exact Exposition* 2.12.

certain extent, in the activities and states of the soul, and vice versa. For example, the body contributes by its words, actions, attitudes, and expressions to our love for God or neighbor. Our humility, our kindness, our inner peace, our spiritual sadness or joy—all are reflected by our bodily attitudes and our facial expressions.

Like Scripture, the Fathers often point out the role played in our spiritual life by the different members of the body.[46] They stress that their purpose is not merely physiological but also one of enabling us, in superlative fashion, to attune ourselves to God and unite ourselves with him. This is above all the case with the senses, which should contribute to our perception of God in all sensible phenomena. Thus, the eyes should enable us to see God in the harmony and beauty of creation[47] and so to praise him and give him thanks.[48] The ears should enable us to "listen to the divine word and God's laws,"[49] but also to hear God in all the world's sounds. The sense of smell should enable us to detect in every creature the "good odor of God" (2 Cor 2.15);[50] the sense of taste to discern in all food "how good the Lord is" (Ps 33.9). The purpose of the other bodily organs is likewise to behave in a godly manner, following St Paul's recommendation: "I beseech you therefore, brethren, by the mercies of God, that you present your bodies a living sacrifice, holy, acceptable to God ..." (Rom 12.1). Thus the spiritual function of the hands is to carry out for and in God whatever is necessary in order to do his will, to act on behalf of justice, to reach out to him in prayer (cf. Ps 87.10; Ps 143.6; Tim 2.8).[51] The task of the feet is to serve God by allowing us to go

---

[46]See Serapion of Thmuis, *Letter to the Monks* 14. Macarius of Egypt, *Letter to his Spiritual Sons*. Nicetas Stethatos, *On Spiritual Knowledge, Love, and the Perfection of Living* 72. Gregory Palamas, *The Triads* 2.2.20.

[47]See Athanasius of Alexandria, *Against the Heathen* 4.

[48]See John Chrysostom, *Homilies on Genesis* 22.3; *Three Homilies Concerning the Power of Demons* 2.3.

[49]See Athanasius of Alexandria, *Against the Heathen* 4.

[50]See Serapion of Thmuis, *Letter to the Monks* 14.

[51]See Macarius of Egypt, *Letter to his Spiritual Sons*. Serapion of Thmuis, *Letter to the Monks* 14. Athanasius of Alexandria, *Against the Heathen* 4. John Chrysostom, *Homilies on Genesis* 22.3; *Three Homilies Concerning the Power of Demons* 2.3. Gregory Palamas, *The Triads* 2.2.20.

to where we may do good.[52] The tongue should proclaim the Good News and sing of God's glory. The heart is to be the place of prayer; the lungs are to produce the breath that regulates and supports it.

Although not always presenting us with such an ideal portrayal—one in which the senses become spiritual senses,[53] the various organs symbolizing the members of the "glorious body" (Phil 3.21), and the body in its entirety having become a "mystical" body—Christian anthropology never loses sight of the nature, purpose, and spiritual value of the body in general and of each of its organs in particular. It is noteworthy that in the Christian portrayal of the body—as Scripture abundantly testifies—the organs always have a more than physiological dimension and their functions are always considered not simply as strictly organic, but spiritual as well.[54] In short, they are never envisaged as independent realities, but always as being in a certain relationship to God.

At the same time, the Fathers refer to the spiritual benefits that our body obtains from being directed towards God in this way; for, acting under the direction of the soul and in collaboration with it, the body too receives the grace of the Holy Spirit. "For as God created the sky and the earth as a dwelling place for man," notes St Macarius of Egypt, "so he also created man's body and soul as a fit dwelling for himself to dwell in and take pleasure in the body, having for a beautiful bride the beloved soul, made according to his own image."[55] This is simply to repeat in another form St Paul's assertion that the body is the "temple of the Holy Spirit" (1 Cor 6.19).

---

[52]See Macarius of Egypt, *Letter to his Spiritual Sons*. Serapion of Thmuis, *Letter to the Monks* 14. John Chrysostom, *Homilies on Genesis* 22.3; *Three Homilies Concerning the Power of Demons* 2.3. Gregory Palamas, *The Triads* 2.2.20.

[53]On this topic, see K. Rahner, "Le début d'une doctrine des cinq sens spirituels chez Origène," *Revue d'ascétique et de mystique* 13 (1932): 113–145.

[54]See M. Andronikof, *Transplantation d'organes et éthique chrétienne: l'éthique, la mort et le corps dans une perspective orthodoxe* (Suresnes: Éditions de l'Ancre, 1993), 70–74.

[55]Macarius of Egypt, *Homilies* 49.4.

5. *Deification, the Body's Spiritual Destiny.*

By this indwelling of divine grace, the body is transformed along
with the soul. In its most elevated form—the one known by the
saints—this transformation becomes *theosis* (deification, diviniza-
tion)—a state in which, while remaining fully human, man becomes
god by grace. Thus, as St Gregory Palamas writes:

> There are indeed blessed passions and common activities of
> body and soul, which ... serve to draw the flesh to a dignity
> close to that of the spirit, and persuade it too to tend towards
> what is above. Such spiritual activities ... do not enter the mind
> from the body, but descend into the body from the mind, in
> order to transform the body into something better and to deify
> it. ... In spiritual man, the grace of the Spirit, transmitted to
> the body through the soul, grants to the body also the experi-
> ence of things divine and allows it the same blessed experiences
> as the soul undergoes. ... When the soul pursues this blessed
> activity, it deifies the body also; which, being no longer driven by
> corporeal and material passions ... rejects all contact with evil
> things. Indeed it inspires its own sanctification and inalienable
> divinization.[56]

St Macarius of Egypt and St Maximus the Confessor also
emphasize in a particularly strong manner that the body is called
to be ultimately divinized along with the soul, in a way that corresponds to it.[57]

It is clear, then, that the importance and dignity accorded the
body from its very beginning in the divine act of creation is seen
again in the ultimate spiritual destiny assigned to it by God, the
former finding in the latter its rationale and its meaning.

---

[56]*Gregory Palamas: The Triads* 2.2.12, N. Gendle, trans. (Mahwah, NJ: Paulist
Press, 1983), 51–52.

[57]See Macarius of Egypt, *Homilies* 15.38. Maximus the Confessor, *Various Texts
on Theology, the Divine Economy, and Virtue and Vice* 2.88.

6. *The Body's Condition in Paradise.*

This destiny Adam (representing all humanity) began to realize in paradise. His body made its own contribution, participating in his sanctification in two ways: in the sense that it actively collaborated with the soul in living a virtuous life, so as to realize the divine plan; but it also participated in the sense that, through these spiritual dispositions, it too received divine grace along with the soul.

The body was not an object of pleasure, nor a means of wielding power over creatures or of selfishly enjoying the world. Its organs were entirely at the service of doing God's will. Its senses were the faithful servants of Adam's spirit, which contemplated God's presence and activity in the world and discerned beneath the perceptible appearances of creatures their inner essence so as, with them, to offer thanks to their Creator.[58] For since he was conceived of by God as a microcosm and established as mediator between himself and creation,[59] Adam's body contributed to the spiritual task of uniting in himself the polarities of creation in order to offer it, unified and sanctified, back to God.[60]

Being transparent to the divine energies, his body benefitted from the blessed action of the grace present in it. His soul—so the Fathers emphasize—was exempt from every passion, and his body from all sickness and suffering, as well as from corruption and death.[61] He was impassible, incorruptible and immortal[62]—not by

[58]See Maximus the Confessor, *Questions to Thalassius* 51.

[59]This is one of the basic themes of St Maximus the Confessor's thinking.

[60]See Maximus the Confessor, *Ambigua* 41.

[61]See Wis 1.13–14. Basil of Caesarea, *Homily Explaining that God is Not the Cause of Evil.* Gregory of Nyssa, *The Great Catechism* 5.8, 8.15; *Letter To Eustathia, Ambrosia, and Basilissa*; *Homilies on the Beatitudes* 3.6; *On Virginity* 12. John Chrysostom, *Homilies on the Statues* 11.2. Maximus the Confessor, *Questions to Thalassius* 21, 41, 42, 61. Gregory Palamas, *The Homilies* 31; *Topics of Natural and Philosophical Science and on the Moral and Ascetic Life* 47, 51.

[62]See Athanasius of Alexandria, *Against the Heathen* 2 and 3. Basil of Caesarea, *Homily Explaining that God is Not the Cause of Evil* 7. Gregory of Nyssa, *The Great Catechism* 5.6.8 and 8.4–5; *On the Making of Man* 4, 17; *On Virginity* 12. John Chrysostom, *Homilies on the Statues* 11.2. John of Damascus, *An Exact Exposition* 2.12.

nature, but by the grace[63] that God had communicated to his entire
being in creating him[64] and that he had preserved by a mode of
existence freely directed towards God and attuned to his will.[65]

By virtue of this grace, the first man's condition was different
from the human condition such as we know it today.[66] Even the
constitution of his body was different from that of the present-day
human body.[67] Whilst noting that it is scarcely possible for us to
imagine what this would have been like, starting from the fallen
state in which we now find ourselves,[68] the Fathers nevertheless
consider that it was similar to the angelic state.[69] For St Maximus
the Confessor[70] and St Gregory of Nyssa, the body of the first
Adam did not possess the materiality, the density, the heaviness, or
the opacity that it does at present. Its constitution was not unlike
that of the resurrection body referred to by St Paul (cf. 1 Cor 15). In
this connection, it is significant that the Fathers think of the post-
resurrection condition of the body as a reintegration of that which
it enjoyed in paradise.[71]

[63]See Athanasius of Alexandria, *Against the Heathen* 2; *On the Incarnation* 5.1–3.
Basil of Caesarea, *Homily Explaining that God is Not the Cause of Evil* 7; *Long Rules*
55. Maximus the Confessor, *On the Lord's Prayer*; *Questions to Thalassius* Prologue.
Gregory Palamas, *The Homilies* 36, 54; *Topics of Natural and Philosophical Science and
on the Moral and Ascetic Life* 46.
[64]In *Homily* 57 Gregory Palamas interprets the breath of life that was breathed
into man's face by the Creator as being the Divine Spirit.
[65]See Theophilus of Antioch, *To Autolycus* 2.27. Athanasius of Alexandria, *On the
Incarnation* 3.4. John Chrystostom, *Homilies on Genesis* 17.7. Maximus the Confessor,
Questions to Thalassius 61. John of Damascus, *An Exact Exposition* 2.11, 30. Gregory
Palamas, *The Homilies* 29, 31, 54, 57; *Topics of Natural and Philosophical Science and on
the Moral and Ascetic Life* 51.
[66]See Gregory of Nyssa, *The Great Catechism* 5.9.
[67]See Maximus the Confessor, *Ambigua* 45.
[68]See Gregory of Nyssa, *The Great Catechism* 5.9.
[69]See John Chrystostom, *Homilies on Genesis* 16.1.
[70]See Maximus the Confessor, *Ambigua* 45.
[71]See Theophilus of Antioch, *To Autolycus* 2.26. Basil of Caesarea, *On the Origin
of Humanity* 2.7. Gregory of Nyssa, *On the Making of Man* 17, 21; *On the Soul and the
Resurrection* 125. Maximus the Confessor, *Questions to Thalassius* 61.

CHAPTER TWO

The Body in Its Fallen State

In paradise, as we have seen, Adam was united to God with his whole being. Transparent to God's energies, he was radiant with grace in both soul and body. As gradually—through partaking of the divine blessings, and commensurate with his spiritual progress—he began to attain the divine likeness, the image of God in which he had been created (body and soul) shone forth, causing him to experience intense pleasure. However, this first state was short-lived.[1] Ceasing to fulfill God's will and turning aside from him, by his own fault he lost the grace he had been receiving and the good things associated with it. The Fathers call this the "ancestral sin"—a sin that was to have a decisive influence on the history of humanity, and whose nature, significance, and consequences enable us to understand much of our present situation, in particular the condition of the body as it is today.

1. *The Role of the Body in Ancestral Sin.*

In this sin, the principal role was played by Adam's spirit. More often than not, the Fathers consider that it was a question of pride: the first man—destined indeed to become god by God's grace—wished to become god by his own means. In other words, he attempted to deify himself, putting his trust in the promise of the serpent: "Ye [will] be as gods" (Gen 3.6).[2] The Fathers also see it as a transgression that Adam committed by the misuse of his intelligence (in ignoring the

---

[1] See Maximus the Confessor, *Questions to Thalassius* 59, 61.

[2] See Irenaeus of Lyons, *Against the Heresies* 5.3.1. John Chrysostom, *Homilies on the Statues* 11.2. John of Damascus, *An Exact Exposition* 2.30. Symeon the New Theologian, *Ethical Discourses* 13.60.

true God[3]) and of his will (in choosing to turn aside from him). But
in this personal sin of Adam's, all of his soul's faculties played a part:
his memory no longer remembered God, his imagination imagined
that which was evil, his appetitive or desiring power coveted false
goods, and his irascible power began to struggle to obtain and hold
on to them, whilst opposing and resisting God's will.

Nevertheless, the body also played an important part. A popular
version of Western Christianity has often portrayed the sin of Adam
and Eve as being one of greed or as sexual in nature, both interpre-
tations being symbolized by the eating of the forbidden fruit. The
Fathers, however, have a more complex view of this incident, though
one which still allots a key role to covetousness and pleasure. The
movement by which we turn away from God goes hand in hand, in
fact, with that by which we turn to sensible things in order to enjoy
them. Each implies the other: we turn to sensible reality because we
have turned aside from God; we drift away from God because we
allow ourselves to be attracted by sensible reality. It remains nonetheless the case that the body plays an essential role in the second of
these movements: We consider the reality of the world, and especially our own body—which is that part of sensible reality that is
the most immediate, the most present, the closest, the most directly
accessible—no longer according to the contemplative activity of
our spirit, but through our senses alone, to which our intelligence
and our other faculties are henceforth subordinate. The pleasure and
pain that we experience in our own body become, as a consequence,
the main criteria by which we judge the value of things.[4] Creatures
are no longer contemplated by our spirit according to their spiritual
essences (their *logoi*) and are no longer related to their Creator, but
are perceived by our senses in their most outward and material form.
In other words, according to their physical appearance, as objects of
sensual pleasure. The body itself becomes the favored instrument of

[3]See Maximus the Confessor, *Questions to Thalassius* Prologue.

[4]See Athanasius of Alexandria, *Against the Heathen* 4. Gregory of Nyssa, *On the Making of Man* 20. Maximus the Confessor, *Questions to Thalassius* Prologue. Gregory Palamas, *The Triads* 2.3.76.

this fleshly pleasure that from now on replaces the spiritual pleasure Adam and Eve had begun to know in paradise and that they were destined to experience in all its fullness.

This impassioned attitude by which we become attached to our own body on account of the pleasure we get from it is called *philautia* by St Maximus the Confessor and other Fathers. *Philautia* can be defined in general terms as the egotistical, passionate love of oneself. But St Maximus stresses the fact that it is rooted in the body, originating and developing in our attachment to it: "Self-love is an impassioned, mindless love for one's body."[5] As a result, the body becomes an idol that man worships.[6] According to St Maximus, it is from *philautia* that proceed all the other passions that appear in the soul and body of fallen man, taking the place of the virtues and developing in their stead. One group of passions stems from the search for pleasure; a second from the avoidance of, or flight from, pain; and a third from a combination of these two tendencies.[7]

Thus the passions that develop in fallen humanity—and which are all pathological forms of attachment to sensible reality and to oneself—involve soul and body simultaneously, though in varying proportions, by reason of the very close links between them. Some—such as pride, vanity, dejection, or *acedia* [listlessness, despondency—*Tr.*]—affect the soul more; others—such as gluttony or the sexual passions—involve the body more; yet others—such as avarice, cupidity or anger—affect both soul and body more or less equally.[8]

The Fathers note, moreover, that it is through the body in particular—for it is the body that experiences them most intensely—that fallen man becomes a prisoner of pleasure and of pain, as well as of the link between them (since they give rise to each other and often follow

[5]Maximus the Confessor, *Centuries on Love* 3.8. See also *Questions to Thalassius* Prologue.

[6]See Maximus the Confessor, *Questions to Thalassius* Prologue.

[7]Ibid.

[8]A detailed account of these various passions can be found in our *Therapy of Spiritual Illnesses: An Introduction to the Ascetic Tradition of the Orthodox Church*, 3 vols., Kilian Sprecher, trans. (Montreal, QC: Alexander Press, 2012). See vol. 1, Part Two.

on from each other, as Plato had already observed[9]). It is on this basis now that we all instinctively decide upon our choices and actions.[10]

It is not that the Fathers have a pejorative view of the body or of pleasure. Rather, they are lamenting their degeneration, following the sin of the first man. For, as we have seen, in their eyes the body enjoys considerable value and is destined for great things, on condition, all the same, that it remain subject to the spirit and transparent to the divine energies in a way of life that is attuned to God's will. The Fathers likewise acknowledge the great value of pleasure and even consider that we were formed by the Creator in such a way that we might seek and enjoy it.[11] But they have in mind here the spiritual pleasure that comes from the enjoyment of the divine blessings, culminating in the highest form of happiness: bliss, the form Christ refers to as "my joy" and of which he wishes his disciples to be "full"(Jn 15.11). In paradise—the word *Eden* itself signifies "delight"[12]—it was this kind of enjoyment that Adam experienced, and it alone. Which is why the Fathers say that he knew neither pain nor, in the limited sense of the word, pleasure, these both having first made their appearance after sin. The pleasure to which Adam yields after his transgression is thus a fallen, inferior form of enjoyment—a cruder form of pleasure, superficial, limited, and of short duration. It takes the place of, and deprives him of, a higher form, one that was more profound, longer lasting,[13] and that he enjoyed more harmoniously with his whole being.

We have seen that, in sinning, Adam turned away from God to turn instead to sensible reality. In so doing he brought about a veritable perversion of all his faculties—those of his soul, but also those of his bodily organs.[14] Instead of being subject to the spirit so as to contribute to the fulfilling of God's will and to establishing a life in

[9]See the beginning of the *Phaedo*.
[10]Freud's pleasure principle is based on a similar notion.
[11]See Maximus the Confessor, *Questions to Thalassius* 61; *On the Lord's Prayer*.
[12]As Gregory of Nyssa reminds us in *On the Making of Man* 19.
[13]See John Chrysostom, *Homilies on Genesis* 1.4.
[14]See Macarius of Egypt, *Homilies* 2.2. Athanasius of Alexandria, *Against the Heathen* 5.

God, they became subject to the senses and now serve to realize, to sustain, and to develop the passions that henceforth inhabit fallen man,[15] and consequently to perform all kinds of evil.[16]

2. *The Effects of Ancestral Sin on the Body.*

For Adam and Eve the effects of their sin were tragic.

Adam turned away from God, and as a result, of his own free will he deprived himself of God's grace, and so he found himself to be deprived also of all the blessings he owed to that grace.[17] Consequently (since evil results from the privation of good[18]), he introduced into himself, into the world, and into all his descendants "a like number of opposite evils."[19]

In the first instance, these evils affected the soul, which became passible, experienced sorrow and suffering, became corrupt, and died a spiritual death through being separated from God and deprived of divine life.[20] They then spread to the body where they manifested themselves in the most sensible manner. From then on, the body became subject to suffering, sickness, corruption, and eventually death.[21]

[15]See Maximus the Confessor, *Questions to Thalassius* 50. Isaac the Syrian, *Ascetical Homilies* 1.

[16]Athanasius of Alexandria, *Against the Heathen* 5.

[17]See Gregory of Nyssa, *The Great Catechism* 5.11. John Chrysostom, *Homilies on Genesis* 16.4. John of Damascus, *An Exact Exposition* 2.30. Gregory Palamas, *Topics of Natural and Philosophical Science and on the Moral and Ascetic Life* 46, 48, 66.

[18]See Dionysius the Areopagite, *On the Divine Names* 5.19–35.

[19]Gregory of Nyssa, *The Great Catechism*, 8.19; see also 5.11; Basil of Caesarea, *Homily Explaining that God is Not the Cause of Evil* 7. Maximus the Confessor, *Ambigua* 10.

[20]See John Chrysostom, *Homilies on the Statues* 11.2. Gregory Palamas, *To the Most Reverend Nun Xenia*; *Homilies*, 11; *Topics of Natural and Philosophical Science and on the Moral and Ascetic Life* 51.

[21]See Romans 5.12. Irenaeus of Lyons, *Against the Heresies* 5.15.2, 5.38.4. Athanasius of Alexandria, *On the Incarnation* 3.4–5, 4.4, 5.1–3. Basil of Caesarea, *Homily Explaining that God is Not the Cause of Evil* 7. Gregory of Nyssa, *The Great Catechism* 8.4; *On the Making of Man* 20; *On the Soul and the Resurrection* 126; *On Virginity* 12. John Chrysostom, *Homilies on Genesis* 17.7; *Homilies on the Statues* 11.2. Cyril of Alexandria, *Commentary on the Epistle to the Romans*, PG 74:789B. Maximus the Confessor, *On the Lord's Prayer*; *Questions to Thalassius* 42, 61; *Ambigua* 7, 10; *Various*

Human nature was now "subject to abnormal conditions."[22] "Men no longer remained as they had been created."[23] Whereas his nature's original mode of existence brought Adam closer to the angelic state, this new mode brought him closer to that of the animals.[24] His body acquired a materiality,[25] a thickness,[26] and an opacity [27] that it did not originally possess. It entered the mainstream of animal, sensible life, and ever since it undergoes the movements, instability, divisions, and oppositions of which his original constitution had no experience.[28] This new mode of existence is indicated in Genesis by the "garments of skin" (Gen 3.22), which symbolize both its material, animal character, the mortality inherent in it, and also the fact that it is, as it were, added on to man's true nature.[29]

As a consequence of ancestral sin, the body has become somewhat objectified, reified. Inasmuch as man makes of it an instrument of pleasure, a means of satisfying his passions, he thereby makes of it an object whose personal and spiritual dimension he denies, ranking it among other material objects.

Moreover, between soul and body fallen man experiences a state of dissociation. Though, from a certain perspective, the soul's subjection to the urges of the body causes it to become attached to it in a new way to the extent that it may even become its slave, from another point of view the body becomes in some measure extraneous

---

Texts on Theology, the Divine Economy, and Virtue and Vice 3.18; *Letter* 10. John of Damascus, *An Exact Exposition* 2.30, 3.1. Gregory Palamas, *To the Most Reverend Nun Xenia*; *Topics of Natural and Philosophical Science and on the Moral and Ascetic Life* 46, 50, 51; *Homilies* 11, 31.

[22] Gregory of Nyssa, *The Great Catechism* 5.11.

[23] Athanasius of Alexandria, *On the Incarnation* 4.1. The translation quoted is by John Behr (Crestwood, NY: St Vladimir's Seminary Press, 2011), 59.

[24] See Maximus the Confessor, *Ambigua* 42. Gregory of Nyssa, *On the Soul and the Resurrection* 126.

[25] See Maximus the Confessor, *Ambigua* 45.

[26] See John of Damascus, *An Exact Exposition*, 3.1. Maximus the Confessor, *Ambigua* 45.

[27] See John of Damascus, *An Exact Exposition*, 3.1.

[28] See Maximus the Confessor, *Ambigua* 45.

[29] See Gregory of Nyssa, *On the Soul and the Resurrection* 126.

to, and alienated from, the soul. The harmony that presided over their relations is largely broken.

All the results of sin that affect the body have the additional consequence of seriously disturbing our relations with our fellow human beings. Fallen man perceives his neighbors first of all through their corporeal reality. Under the influence of the passions, he reduces this reality to a mere matter of physical appearance, no longer experiencing it insofar as it relates to his neighbor's soul and spirit, nor as a dimension of his person. The other then becomes an object of enjoyment and domination; hence the relational difficulties that people unintentionally experience in living together. A good number of philosophers (e.g., Spinoza, Hobbes, Hegel, and Freud) have drawn a bleak picture of this, in their descriptions of what they call man's "natural state." This so-called "natural" state is, in fact, humanity's fallen state, as expressed in society before the existence of any laws designed to regulate relations between its members. Hobbes's famous saying summarizes this state of affairs at its worst: "Man is a wolf to man."

In the conflicts that take place between people, many of the Fathers stress the role played by *philautia*, that mother of all passions whose favored link with the body we have already seen. "O what proceeds from a self-love that hates all!" cry one after the other Evagrius,[30] St Theodore of Edessa,[31] and St John of Damascus.[32] St Maximus the Confessor, for his part, underlines the divisive character of this mother of all passions: "Because of it, human nature disintegrated into a thousand fragments";[33] "it is this that caused us to stray away from God and our fellow men,... that cut up the single nature into many pieces";[34] that, "out of love of pleasure, caused us to direct our aggressive power—now become ferocious—against each other";[35] that "brutified the most sociable of natures and dissected

[30]Evagrius Ponticus, *Maxims* 2.24.

[31]See Theodore of Edessa (Theodoros the Great Ascetic), *A Century of Spiritual Texts* 93.

[32]See John of Damascus, *Sacred Parallels* 13.

[33]Maximus the Confessor, *Questions to Thalassius* Introduction.

[34]Maximus the Confessor, *Letter* 27; see also *Letter* 2.

[35]Maximus the Confessor, *Letter* 27.

humanity, in essence one, into many antagonistic and mutually destructive parts."[36] Where *philautia* reigns one sees nothing but opposition, division, rivalry, envy, jealousy, dissension, hostility, quarrels, and aggressiveness. All of these are the fruits of this one passion, as are antisocial behavior, injustice, the many forms of exploitation, slavery, torture, rape, murder, wars, and so on.[37]

3. *The Body's Role in Transmitting the Effects of Ancestral Sin.*

The consequences of the sin of our first parents also affected the entire universe: "Cursed is the ground for thy sake," (Gen 3.17) said God to Adam, announcing the cosmic catastrophe produced by his transgression. For man had been established as king of creation (Gen 1.28–30) and mediator between it and God.[38] They also spread to the whole of humanity, since Adam was its prototype and "root,"[39] and since all human beings are his descendants.[40] As this transmission is perpetuated biologically[41] from generation to generation, we all inherit at birth Adam's fallen nature—a nature that is sick, infirm, and marked by the consequences of his sin.[42] As St Gregory of Nyssa explains:

> Evil is mixed up with our nature through those who by disobedience gave house-room to the disease.[43] Just as with each kind of animal the species continues along with the succession of the new generation, so that what is born is, following a natural design, the same as those from which it is born, . . . so

[36]Maximus the Confessor, *Questions to Thalassius* 40.

[37]See Clement of Alexandria, *The Instructor*, 3.2. Theodoret of Cyrus, *On Divine Providence* 7. Maximus the Confessor, *On the Lord's Prayer.* John of Damascus, *Sacred Parallels* 13.

[38]See Gregory of Nyssa, *On the Making of Man* 4; *The Great Catechism* 6.10. Maximus the Confessor, *Letters* 10. John of Damascus, *An Exact Exposition* 2.30.

[39]See Gregory of Nyssa, *On the Making of Man* 16, 22. Mark the Monk, *On the Incarnation* 18; Gregory Palamas, *Homilies* 5, 52.

[40]See Maximus the Confessor, *Questions to Thalassius* 61; *Ambigua 10.*

[41]See Theodoret of Cyrus, *Commentary on the Epistle to the Romans.* Maximus the Confessor, *Questions to Thalassius* 21, 61. John of Damascus, *An Exact Exposition* 2.30. Gregory Palamas, *Homilies* 5.

[42]See Maximus the Confessor, *Questions to Thalassius* 21, 61.

[43]The word is to be understood here in a general sense.

from man man is generated, from passion passionate, from the sinful its like.[44]

We see here that the Fathers consider there to be a link between ancestral sin and sexuality. Not in the sense that the former was brought about by the latter (as is often thought to be the case in a popular form of Western Christianity), but in that sexuality first appeared after, and as a result of, the sin of our first parents. Whilst taking a negative view of sexuality insofar as it is the means by which humans transmit to each other the effects of ancestral sin, the Fathers also have a positive view; for it is seen to be the providential means given by God to man—now become mortal—to ensure the survival of the race.[45]

4. *The Body, a Subject of Contradiction.*

The above references to Adam—to his condition in paradise, followed by his fallen state—might seem to be outdated, to belong to the field of myth or, worse, legend. Surely science has long since done away with this account and made it pointless.

It is true that, strictly speaking, it is an account that does not belong to history, but rather to what might be styled meta-history.

On the one hand, time in paradise and at the fall was not time as we know it now—the time studied by historians, designated in Greek by the word *chronos*—but a time that had more extension, being made up of sequences of length of much longer duration, and that the Fathers refer to by the word *aeon*. This latter term—frequently found in theological and liturgical language—is often translated as "age" (for example, in the phrase "unto ages of ages"). Though inadequate, this translation allows us to understand, symbolically, that one second of our time is, as it were, a whole "age" in that other time. The time of the *aeons* is in a sense intermediate

---

[44]Gregory of Nyssa, *Homilies on the Beatitudes* 6.5. See Maximus the Confessor, *Questions to Thalassius* 61 (PG 632A); Gregory Palamas, *Homilies* 43, 54.

[45]In fact, in the opinion of several Fathers, humans were required to reproduce even before the fall, in obedience to the divine command—"Be fruitful and multiply; fill the earth . . ." (Gen 1.28)—though in a manner that was not sexual. See Maximus the Confessor, *Questions and Doubts*, 1.3; *Ambigua* 41.

between our present time and eternity. After sinning, the first man entered time as we know it now, which is fallen time, the time that history deals with. Something of the ancient modality of time, however, is preserved at the beginning of history, where the Bible shows the first men as having lived for several centuries.

On the other hand, the story of the first man—his creation, his sin, and his fall—is less a historical account set in the physical world, than one that is metaphysical or spiritual. Without belonging, strictly speaking, to the category of myth—for it is not without a basis in reality—it is nonetheless similar, by being situated in a time that precedes time strictly defined ("at that time, in those days"), by its powerful symbolism, and above all by its explanatory value on an existential and spiritual level.[46]

Although distant and set in a time that for us is different and indefinite—that of the origins—the story of Adam and Eve retains exemplary value and enables us to gain a deep understanding of what we are. In particular, it allows us to understand the many contradictions that we experience in relation to our body, as mentioned in our Introduction. Blaise Pascal—no doubt the philosopher who felt these contradictions most intensely—did not fail, when seeking their causes, to refer to the double "origin" of man.[47] In conformity with the state in which it was created—in the image of God, an image that continues to exist in the present nature of each of us—our body still possesses certain qualities, the most obvious being its harmonious organization and beauty. For the body is indeed still a body of beauty, "the temple of the Holy Spirit" (1 Cor 6.19) and potentially a "glorious body" (Phil 3.21), being the faithful servant of our spirit's good intentions. But at the same time, in conformity with its fallen state, the body is prone to suffering, sickness, and death. We feel its tensions, its needs, its urges, some of which lead us to commit evil. It is then a "body of sin" (Rom 6.6), a "body of death" (Rom 7.24).[48]

[46]See Mircea Eliade, *Myth and Reality*, W. Trask, trans. (New York: Harper and Row, 1963).

[47]Pascal, *Pensées*, pp. 149–151.

[48]It is a paradox summed up in the title of Olivier Clément's book *Corps de mort et de gloire* (Paris: Desclée de Brouwer, 1995).

CHAPTER THREE

The Body Saved and Deified
by the Incarnate Word

1. *The Incarnation.*

Through the incarnation of the Word, the Son of God, the human body is both rehabilitated and accorded supreme value. In making the incarnation one of the fundamental tenets of its faith, one of its basic principles, Christianity—of all religions—is seen to be the one that accords most importance and value to the body, destining it for the highest of callings.

The incarnation means that God himself, in the person of his Son, took not only a human spirit and soul but also a human body. It should be noted that the very etymology of this traditional term "incarnation"—usually employed in a general, overall sense to mean that the Son of God became man, assuming human nature in its fullness, even in its fallen state (excepting sin and the culpable passions)—puts particular stress on the fact that God took a body, that he became flesh.

That God should become human was something unheard of for the religions and philosophies of antiquity, even more so that he should take an actual body: "to the Jews a stumbling block and to the Greeks foolishness" (1 Cor 1.23).

In the eyes of the Fathers, the virginal conception and birth of Christ imply no disdain for marriage or the usual means of conception and birth. Rather, they see here a pointer to Christ's freedom from those consequences of ancestral sin that we all inherit in being born: passibility, corruptibility, mortality, and also a certain tendency to commit sin. Not having been conceived or born according to the usual "laws of nature," Christ was thus not subject to these laws, as are other humans. Instead, he experienced the natural and non-culpable passions (hunger, thirst, suffering, fear, sorrow, etc.), corruption, and death by freely assuming them in a manner that was totally voluntary. Thus he was able in himself to free us from their tyranny and, more generally, from the domination exercised over us through them by sin and the devil.

2. *The Role of Christ's Body in the Work of Salvation.*

Having a body, then, and experiencing in it all that we experience in ours, Christ is thereby able, through his divine power, to sanctify and glorify what is good about the human body and to burn up what is bad, even as he does for our soul.

With considerable realism, the Gospels show us that it is by means of his body as well that Christ accomplishes our salvation.

For example, in the desert during the three temptations, to which he voluntarily exposes himself so as to vanquish them and enable us in turn to be victorious over them, one is struck by the significant role his body plays—whether it be experiencing hunger, the temptation to throw himself from the pinnacle of the temple, or to bow down before the devil (cf. Mt 4.1–11; Lk 4.1–13). Clearly, his body also plays an essential role in the saving suffering of the passion and cross.

St Maximus the Confessor shows how the passibility affecting fallen human beings in body and soul constitutes a point of weakness that the demons make use of in order to tempt us and lure us into giving way to evil passions—one group being linked to the quest for pleasure, another to the avoidance of pain, and a third to a combination of these two tendencies. He also shows how Christ overthrew the tyranny exercised over our nature in this way by the demons; and in particular, he does this in the two major episodes of his saving work, situated respectively at the beginning and the end of his public life: his sojourn in the desert, and his passion. In the desert, by resisting unflinchingly those temptations relative to the attraction of pleasure, he acquired for us the power to conquer all the passions linked to this tendency. During his passion and on the cross, showing himself to be inflexible when faced with those temptations linked to the avoidance of pain, he acquired for us the power to be able to escape from the passions relative to this other tendency.[1]

But it was also when he was working miracles that Christ's body played an important role. Following St Cyril of Alexandria, St Maximus places great emphasis on the fact that a given miracle is not accomplished simply by order of Christ's divine will or by the all-powerful energy that is his as God, but also by his voice and by contact with his human flesh.[2]

3. *"Take, eat; this is my body."*

It is particularly typical that, when Christ wishes to make his believers his participants in the most profound and intimate manner and to make them share in what he is, he gives them as food his own body and his own blood (cf. Mt 26.26–28; Mk 14.22–24; Lk 22.19–20). In communicating with the body and blood of Christ, the believer also communicates with his soul and spirit—in short, with the entire person of Christ. Here, confirmed by Christ himself, can be seen on the one hand the essential link that unites body, soul, and spirit in the human being; and on the other the fact that the body involves the entire person. Moreover, in Christ's case—since his human nature is united to his divine nature—communion with his body implies communion with the divine nature, and thus not simply with the person of the Word but with the persons of the Father and of the Holy Spirit, since the divine nature is one, and common to the three divine persons.[3]

---

[1] See Maximus the Confessor, *Questions to Thalassius* 21.

[2] See Maximus the Confessor, *Theological and Polemical Opuscules* 7, 8, 9.

[3] It is worth noting that the liturgy of St John Chrysostom specifically states that whoever is about to partake of the body and blood of Christ by that fact also partakes of the Holy Spirit. [See, for example, the priest's secret prayers following the consecration.—*Trans.*]

4. *The Transfiguration.*

The close union of Christ's human and divine natures in his person
is made vividly manifest during his transfiguration, when the eyes of
those apostles present were suddenly opened by the Holy Spirit so
that they were able to see his body become transparent to the divine
energies; and when, through his body, Christ's human nature was
shown to be bathed in them, filled, enveloped, and totally permeated by them. Through the transfiguration, for those deemed worthy,
the possibility now exists of seeing, in the uncreated divine light,
Christ glorified even in his body, and also, since such people are intimately united to Christ, the possibility of themselves receiving and
manifesting by grace this same light that he possesses by nature, and
which radiates from him. Thus the transfiguration bears witness in
striking fashion not simply to Christ's divine-humanity, to the close
union and compenetration in his person of his two natures (divine
and human), but also to our own vocation to be deified by grace in
our whole being, including our bodies.

   The transfiguration, then, as well as the Eucharist, demonstrates
the supreme spiritual value that is bestowed on the human body by
Christ himself. These two events clearly show that in Christ there
"dwells all the fullness of the Godhead *bodily*" (Col 2.9). They also
reveal—in advance—the pre-eminent value accorded the body of
every believer who partakes of Christ in communion, thus becoming
"in his likeness" and, by grace, a bearer of the divine energies.

5. *Death and Resurrection.*

Christ's death on the cross, where he "himself bore our sins in his
own body" (1 Pet 2.24), results from God's wish to set mankind free
from the grip of sin and the tyranny of the devil which, ever since
Adam's transgression, had subjugated them, vanquished them by
death, and kept them captives of hell. It also testifies to a wish to
deliver the body from corruption, dissolution, and eternal death.
Here, too, we must stress along with St Paul the paramount role

played by Christ's body in the work of salvation and the potential deification of all human beings: "We have been sanctified through the offering of the body of Jesus Christ once for all" (Heb 10.10).

Christ's resurrection bears witness to this liberation, this victory that he acquired definitively for all people, and in which eternal life is bestowed not just on the soul but also on the body.

After his resurrection, Christ's body manifests the characteristics that will be those of our own bodies after our resurrection and that were to some extent those of the bodies of our first parents in paradise. It has attained a spiritual mode of existence. It is different in appearance (cf. Mk 16.12), to the extent that the disciples are unable to recognize it (cf. Jn 21.4; Lk 24.16, 37), and it no longer need obey the laws of physics. Thus it is able to enter a room whose doors are all closed (cf. Jn 20.19, 26), to manifest itself in several different places at once (cf. Mk 16.9–14), or to make itself invisible to those at his side (cf. Lk 24.31).[4] Nevertheless, his body is still a human body, and is indeed still his own body (cf. Lk 24.39–40; Jn 20.27).

6. *The Ascension.*

The ascension of Christ into heaven is further evidence of this new state of the human body, capable now of escaping the law of gravity—something that is also demonstrated, on their own level, by the levitation of certain mystics. But this final episode of Christ's earthly life clearly has deeper significance: namely, that of the risen body's access to the eternal life of the kingdom of heaven; of man's glorification, too, now that his entire being has been saved, both soul and body. In his person, Christ raises humanity—whose entire nature is now saved and deified—to make it a participant in the life of the Trinity, thereby establishing the possibility for all human beings to have a similar spiritual destiny.

---

[4]Though he takes food in the company of his disciples (Lk 24.41–43), this is not out of necessity but economy, lest they should think it is a ghost that has appeared to them (cf. Mk 6.49; Lk 24.37).

It is a destiny that corresponds to God's original plan in creating man and which has always remained his plan, despite man's fall. Christ came to accomplish fully that which the first humans began to realize but which, through their own fault, they were unable to complete.

7. *Christ, Physician of Bodies.*

In the above episodes in Christ's life—during which he accomplished in his person the salvation and deification of the humanity he had assumed—we clearly see how God himself acknowledges the prominent spiritual role and transcendent value of the human body.

This is confirmed in another way by the great attentiveness and extreme compassion Christ shows to those suffering in their body—whether through hunger, thirst, sickness, or infirmity. The numerous accounts of miracles related in the Gospels abundantly illustrate this, as does the fact that—especially in the early period of Christianity—Christ was thought of as the supreme physician, not just of souls but of bodies too.[5] This concern of Christ's, and then of his apostles, for the sick and infirm was surprising at a time when the dominant philosophies and religions tended rather to be concerned with those in good health, attaching importance to the salvation of the soul alone.[6] Christ, however, expressing God's love for mankind, shows that he has come to save man as a whole, both soul and body, and not only in this life, in which he invites us to experience in both body and soul the first fruits of the divine blessings, but also after death in the next world where, after raising our body and making it incorruptible, he intends us to enjoy these blessings in all their fullness with our whole being. In other words, with our whole spirit, our whole soul, and our whole body for all eternity.

---

[5] Cf. our book entitled *The Theology of Illness*, J. and M. Breck, trans. (Crestwood, NY: St Vladimir's Seminary Press, 2002).
[6] Ibid.

The bodily healings performed by Christ are themselves most often signs and symbols of the healing he has come to bring to our whole being, and in the first place, of our spiritual healing. Here once again we see that the human body must not be understood as being simply one constituent part of human nature—admittedly, inseparable from the other two (soul and spirit)—but also as a dimension of the person, something that gives expression to the total person and reflects it in its entirety. Thus, just as to harm the body is to harm the whole person, even so to tend to and heal the body is to take care of the whole person.

By virtue of the fact that, on the one hand, all human beings are made in the image of the Word, and on the other that in becoming man the Word assumed humanity as a whole, any evil done to a human being—not just in soul but in body too—thereby affects Christ himself, just as any good done to a man or woman, whether in body or soul, is directed through them to Christ:

> "Lord, when did we see you hungry and feed you, and thirsty or give you drink? When did we see you a stranger and take you in, or naked and clothe you? Or when did we see you sick, or in prison, and come to you?" . . . "Assuredly, I say to you, inasmuch as you did it to one of the least of these my brethren, you did it to me. . . . Assuredly, I say to you, inasmuch as you did not do it to one of the least of these, you did not do it to me." (Mt 25.34–45)

CHAPTER FOUR

The Body in Spiritual Life

1. *The Christian, Member of the Body of Christ.*

It is within the Church that a Christian personally receives the grace of salvation and deification that was obtained by Christ for all people. Now it is significant that the Church should be conceived of as a body—the body of Christ—and that by being integrated into the Church a Christian becomes a member of Christ's body (cf. 1 Cor 12.27; Eph 5.30). In this way, all Christians together form a single body, which is Christ's (cf. Rom 12.5; 1 Cor 12.12–13) and of which he is the head (cf. Eph 1.23). Thus they become members not simply of Christ but of each other (cf. Rom 12.5); the human nature that had become divided and fragmented by sin regains in Christ its unity. In this body the members each continue to have their own personal distinctive characteristics and gifts (cf. Rom 12.6–8; 1 Cor 12.4–11, 28–30). But the differences between people are no longer a source of opposition, the uniqueness of each is no longer a source of superiority or inferiority or exclusion of others (cf. 1 Cor 12.14–17). Instead, they give rise to a life in which concord and harmony prevail (cf. Eph 4.16), with each member—exactly as in a physical body—having a unique function, irreplaceable, indispensable, complementary, contributing to the life and good of the whole (cf. 1 Cor 12.7, 14–25), and in all things displaying solidarity with others (cf. 1 Cor 12.24–26).

2. *The Body in the Sacraments.*

It is by means of the sacraments that we become members of the Church—Christ's divine-human body—and that we receive the grace acquired for humanity by him during his saving and deifying economy. In other words, in the sacraments we become ontologically related to Christ himself, united to him in real terms by the energy of the Holy Spirit, whom the Church invokes during each sacrament. This grace is communicated to our entire person by means of the visible, material signs that make up the rites and which in the first place are applied to the body.

Thus the body plays a particularly important part in the reception of the sacraments. Once again we see that it represents and expresses the total person, as is especially striking in the ancient forms of Christian rituals—faithfully preserved by the Orthodox Church—in which symbolism is omnipresent, and in which the different bodily organs and functions are related to the organs and functions of the soul, and to the activities and states of the spiritual life. This symbolism, which is extremely rich, cannot be analyzed in detail here.[1] Let us simply call to mind the central act in the service of baptism: the triple immersion in, and the triple emersion from, the baptismal waters, signifying the death of the "old man" and the rising again as a "new man." (The number three symbolizes both the Trinity—which is correlatively invoked at this point—and also the three days spent by Christ in the tomb prior to his resurrection.) Let us mention also the principal rite in the sacrament of chrismation.[2] Saying "the seal of the gift of the Holy Spirit," the priest anoints the baptized person with holy chrism in the sign of the cross successively on the forehead, eyes, nostrils, lips, ears, breast, hands, and feet. Thus, each of the faculties symbolized by these different bodily organs receives the grace that enables the recipient to turn to God and to become whole-heartedly active in a way that conforms to his will, whilst benefitting from the assistance of the Spirit, with his vivifying, sanctifying, illuminating, and deifying energy.

We see that what are also anointed here are the five senses, which are our doors onto the external world and through which sin

[1] A fully developed interpretation can be found in Cyril of Jerusalem's *Mystagogical Catecheses*.

[2] In the Western Church this has been separated from baptism and become the sacrament of confirmation.

had previously gained entry. From now on, with the help of grace, they must be guarded against the intrusion of any evil coming from the "world," and become instead a source for the contemplation of God and the fulfilling of his will. Also anointed are the forehead, symbol of the mind and all the intellectual faculties; secondly the breast, wherein lies the heart, spiritual center of the human being (that Christians must henceforth guard from evil tendencies, feelings, intentions, desires, and movements originating within us and that we must, notably through prayer, make the place of the Spirit); thirdly the hands, which must now serve to carry out God's work; and lastly the feet, which must be used to follow the paths of the Lord. In this way, we discover by grace the ability to make spiritual use of the different faculties of our soul and our different bodily organs, as our first parents were able to do in paradise.

In the Eucharist, the baptized person receives Christ who, in his body and blood, gives himself entirely, not just as man but also as God, since "in him dwells all the fullness of the Godhead" (Col 2.9). Though it is Christ's body that the faithful receive as food, it is his whole being (body, soul, and spirit) that they assimilate. Christ's body spreads to all the bodily members of the communicant and also to all the faculties of the soul, mingling intimately with them.[3] Thus the communicant becomes a "Christ-bearer,"[4] for through communion there is an indwelling of Christ in the Christian and of the Christian in Christ: "He who eats my flesh and drinks my blood abides in me, and I in him" (Jn 6.56). By this sacrament, notes St Gregory of Nyssa, God "infused himself into perishable humanity for this purpose, namely that by this communion with Deity mankind might at the same time be deified."[5] But even before that stage is reached, this spiritual food nourishes, purifies, sustains, fortifies, strengthens, and protects both body and soul against all evil. Though absorbed by the body and bringing into play its digestive

[3]See John Chrysostom, *Homilies on the Gospel of St John* 46.3. This is also confirmed in the post-communion prayers that the faithful should say.
[4]See Cyril of Jerusalem, *Mystagogical Catecheses* 4.3.
[5]Gregory of Nyssa, *The Great Catechism* 37.

functions, it is nonetheless very different from ordinary food, and it is in quite another way that, for the recipient, it is a source of life. As St Nicholas Cabasilas explains, "Man lives because of food, but not in the same way in this sacred rite. Since natural food is not itself living it does not of itself infuse life into us.... But the Bread of Life is himself living, and through him those to whom he imparts himself truly live. While natural food is changed into him who feeds on it . . . here it is entirely opposite. The Bread of Life himself changes him who feeds on him and transforms and assimilates him into himself."[6]

3. *The Body in the Practice of the Virtues.*

Although, in baptism and communion, Christians receive from God the fullness of grace, they must nonetheless assimilate it personally, must grow in it and through it. For this, their own collaboration is required, and it is in leading a spiritual life that this synergy between the strength given by God and their own efforts must be put into practice.

At the initial stage, spiritual life consists in what the Greek Fathers call *praxis*, which is essentially the keeping of God's commandments. Contrary to what is the case in legalistic religions such as Judaism or Islam, these commandments are not laws that we must obey in a formal manner in order to be saved; nor are they rules designed to restrict or reduce our freedom. Rather, taken together, they constitute a way of life that enables us to conform ourselves to Christ and to acquire in him that likeness to God that will ultimately make us partakers of divine life. In other words, keeping the divine commandments should lead us on to the practice of the virtues in imitation of Christ who, by his words and actions, has given us in his own person the perfect example. By means of these virtues, which make us similar to God, we are merely realizing our own potential, that to which our nature destines us and to which we are called by

[6]Nicholas Cabasilas, *The Life in Christ* 4.8, C. J. deCatanzaro, trans. (Crestwood, NY: St Vladimir's Seminary Press, 1974), 125–26.

personal vocation.[7] In fact, as we have seen, the virtues bring into play all of our faculties in a way that conforms to their nature and their normal purpose,[8] and in this sense we find in them our self-fulfillment.

The practice of the virtues requires at the same time effort, hard work, and discipline (called "ascesis" by the Fathers) in order to fight against the passions that have taken their place as a consequence of sin, to reduce their power, and ultimately to eliminate them. The two processes go hand in hand: the more the passions lose their force, the more the virtues increase; the more the virtues develop, the more the passions are weakened. This is due to the fact that passions and virtues both bring into play the same faculties: in the latter case, corresponding to their use in conformity with their nature; in the former, their unnatural use.[9]

In this fight against the passions and the struggle to acquire the virtues, the body plays an essential role, along with the soul. For, as we have seen, soul and body are connected and interdependent, whether it be in realizing the good or in committing evil. Moreover the virtues, like the passions, are common to the body and the soul even if, as mentioned earlier, in different proportions. Thus St Paul invites us to a task of conversion in which he recognizes that the different functions of the body have a key role to play alongside the various faculties of the soul: "And do not present your members as instruments of unrighteousness to sin, but present yourselves to God as being alive from the dead, and your members as instruments of righteousness to God" (Rom 6.13).

In the virtuous life, the soul certainly plays a dominant role, since it is from the soul that proceed those good inclinations and dispositions on which the virtues are founded. Likewise in the combat against the passions, it is the soul that is in a leading position, for the source of the passions lies in evil thoughts and it is in the struggle

---

[7]For a detailed exposition of the virtues, see our *Therapy of Spiritual Illnesses*, vol. 2, Part Four; vol. 3, Parts Five and Six.

[8]See ibid.

[9]See ibid.

against these and in being vigilant in guarding against them that the key to victory lies. But by reason of its close links with the soul, the body can, by its movements or states, further the irruption or multiplication of evil thoughts, can contribute to the implementation and development of the passions, or on the contrary frustrate the production of these evil thoughts, contribute to their weakening and repression, and even help the soul fight them more effectively.

4. *The Meaning of Bodily Asceticism.*

It is the latter goal in particular that is pursued by those who engage in ascetical practices narrowly defined—fasts, vigils, and tiring work. It is not a question of making oneself suffer or of acquiring "merits," as was thought in distorted forms of Western Christian spirituality, but of achieving better control of the body. This enables one to subject it to the spirit, to control its urges, its tendencies, and spiritually undesirable states, and so to weaken the power of the passions and of evil thoughts (which arise in particular from the memory and the imagination, both of which are closely linked to the senses). By these methods one is also able to take advantage of the relationship that the body has with the soul and the influence that its states exert over the soul, so that these may foster its spiritual activity as much as possible. Thus the two-thousand-year old experience of Christian spiritual masters has shown that fasting and vigils significantly help the soul to be more vigilant, to become more perceptive when discerning the nature of the thoughts that arise before it, to use more strength in the fight against temptations, and equally to be more attentive, zealous, and compunctious when praying.

It is these same goals that the Orthodox Church pursues—on a more moderate yet more continuous level—in prescribing abstinence from food and sexual activity on Wednesdays and Fridays[10] and throughout the four annual fasts.[11] Those who make an effort to

---

[10]Days on which, liturgically, the Church commemorates the cross.

[11]The four are: Lent (the Great Fast), leading up to Pascha; the Nativity Fast, preceding Christmas; the Dormition Fast, preceding August 15 when the church

follow the rules progressively develop the virtue of temperance. (See Section 6 below.) They learn—through control of their eating habits and sexual behavior—no longer blindly and unthinkingly to follow these particular bodily urges, which are the strongest of all, being the most closely connected to the vital instincts. In this way, in addition to control of the body and that part of the psyche intimately linked to it, they acquire spiritual independence from the body's needs and states as well as from the pleasure-displeasure principle that is the source of all the passions.[12] As a result, they benefit from greater control of their thoughts, imagination, and desires. Concentration during spiritual activity becomes easier. Penitence—the driving force of spiritual life—humility, and prayer are all fostered, and the body participates in what is the main purpose of these periods of fasting: an intensification of spiritual life, more progress in it, and preparation to receive with profit the grace dispensed during the commemoration of the saving events (or of the saints) that are celebrated by the Church at their close.

5. *The Meaning of Ascetic Control of the Body.*

From another point of view, the progressive control of thoughts and of the various states attained by the soul in its spiritual life also enables a control of the body that is more and more perfect, since, though the soul depends to some extent on the body, the body depends on the soul to a much greater degree.

celebrates the feast of the Dormition of the Mother of God; and the Apostles' Fast, preceding the feast of Sts Peter and Paul on June 29. The rules of abstinence require one to refrain from eating meat, eggs, dairy products, and also—depending on the particular period or day in the calendar—fish, vegetable oils and fats, and wine. These rules are related to the effects such foodstuffs produce in the body and, through it, the psyche. Abstinence is thus more qualitative than quantitative in nature; whereas fasting is more quantitative than qualitative, since it consists in refraining from eating any food at all for a certain period of time, or in limiting the amount consumed, whatever its nature.

[12]See ch. 2 above, p. 33ff. It is important to note that one can derive the same benefits from abstinence even when ill, suffering, or infirm—provided one endures with patience. This is why the rules are still applied—though with more flexibility—to the sick or to those weakened by old age.

Although Christian ascetics may achieve a control of their bodies that can from many points of view be compared to that of a Hindu sage or a Zen Buddhist master, in their case this control is in no sense an end in itself. The aim of Christian asceticism is not to establish inner power, to reveal latent forces in the body and thereby in the soul, to commune with the energy of the cosmos through that of the body, or to enjoy a force drawn from within oneself which produces the impression of one's own powerfulness. The Christian ascetic does not forget the word of God that was addressed to St Paul: "My strength is made perfect in weakness" (2 Cor 12.9). The only true strength is that of grace, which is a gift from God and given only when man recognizes and experiences his own weakness. Now, fasts, vigils, and tiredness (especially when a result of hard work) are precisely means by which we can take the measure of our weakness, our powerlessness, and our ontological inadequacy. Far from turning us in on ourselves, from focusing on ourselves, Christian asceticism opens us up to the Other, without whom we are nothing.

The goal of this control won over the body—in addition to what was said above—is to free us from the ties that, through the body, bind us to the world and to our self (especially through *philautia*, self-love). In other words, to enable us to free ourselves from the passions.

6. *Temperance.*

This control of the body is notably achieved through temperance, which according to the Fathers is one of the four generic virtues— called "cardinal" in the West—that determine the acquisition of all the others. According to St Basil of Caesarea, temperance (or continence) is "the basic principle of spiritual life."[13] Generally speaking, it consists in mastering one's desiring power by inhibiting passionate desires, and by abstaining from the pleasure connected with them. More specifically, it is not simply the control of desires, but also of

[13]Basil of Caesarea, *Long Rules* 17.

all impassioned tendencies, impulses, and movements of the body,[14] and the ability to renounce the pleasures related to them. This is the virtue St Paul demonstrates when he writes, "I discipline my body and bring it into subjection" (1 Cor 9.27). Sometimes the Fathers call this virtuous disposition the "guarding of the body," though it can also be described as the "guarding of the soul," since bodily desires are necessarily linked to those of the soul and often even proceed from them, and since temperance in the broadest sense of the term concerns all forms of passionate desire and pleasure.

Passionate desires are those that cause us to be attached to ourselves and to the things of this world, causing us to turn away from God. So the practice of temperance does not mean the elimination of every form of desire, the renunciation of all use of our desiring power. Rather, it is a matter of eliminating only those desires that are *impassioned*, of renouncing any use of our desiring power that is *against nature*. (Thus St Hermas notes that temperance consists in abstaining from every "*evil* desire."[15]) Nor does the abstention from pleasure that temperance brings about mean that one should renounce every form of enjoyment, but simply the sort of pleasure connected with these types of desire. The "denial of the body," as St Basil defines temperance,[16] does not imply a rejection of the body—by disregarding it, for example, or treating it with disdain—but rather a refusal to become passionately attached to it and to what it covets. As St Gregory Palamas reminds us, commenting on a verse from St Paul (Rom 7.24), "the body is not evil in itself"; what the Apostle is "attacking is not the body, but the sinful desire that entered in because of the Fall."[17]

A passionate desire is such only because, through its object, it aims at sensible pleasure instead of spiritual good. We have seen that no object is evil in itself but that what may well be evil is the goal

---

[14]See ibid. See also his *Letter* 366 (to Urbicius the monk, concerning continence).

[15]*The Shepherd of Hermas*, Vision 3.8.

[16]Basil of Caesarea, *Letter* 366.

[17]Gregory Palamas, *The Triads* 2.2.1, N. Gendle, trans., 41.

we pursue through objects, or the use we make of them. Which is why, as St John Cassian says, it is a question less of abstaining from things themselves so much as of restraining the passionate movements that we may feel towards them and that incite us to seek sensible pleasure.[18]

The central principle of temperance, then, consists in not having pleasure as the objective in our use of things.[19] Temperance uncouples desire from sensible pleasure, prevents it from being a desire *for* pleasure, and in general frees it from all its pathological cathexes.

In this way, temperance can realize its aim of controlling desire, can regain possession of it, submit it to reason,[20] regulate it,[21] and be in command. Which is why the Greek word for temperance (*egkrateia*) can also be translated as "self-control." If temperance frees desire from its alienation to the flesh, putting an end to its impassioned use, it is so as to restore its normal purpose, in conformity with its true nature. In other words, to redirect and channel it definitively towards God and the enjoyment of spiritual good things, an enjoyment far superior in quality and intensity than that of sensible pleasure. Temperance would be pointless, if it did not enable human desire to be refocused on God. As Clement of Alexandria makes clear, "celibacy is not particularly praiseworthy unless it arises through love of God;[22] . . . We embrace self-control out of the love we bear the Lord."[23] In the same vein, St Basil emphasizes that, if temperance is "denial of the body"—according to his own definition, cited above—it is correlatively "to have part with God."[24]

---

[18]See John Cassian, *The Conferences* 5.19.
[19]See Gregory of Nyssa, *On Virginity* 19.
[20]See Clement of Alexandria, *The Stromata 3.7.*
[21]See Maximus the Confessor, *Centuries on Love* 4.15.
[22]Clement of Alexandria, *The Stromata 3.6.51.*
[23]Ibid. 3.7.59.
[24]Basil of Caesarea, *Letter* 366.

7. *Control of Dietary and Sexual Behavior*

The passionate bodily desires that temperance aims to control are in the main those relating to nutrition and sexuality. From what has already been said, it should be evident that there is no suggestion here that either function should be looked down upon or dismissed.

Concerning nutrition, from the outset the Fathers detected its profound links not just with our psychic life but also with our spiritual life. It is well known that extreme forms of eating behavior—whether to excess (as with bulimia) or inadequately (as with anorexia)—involve the underlying relationship the person has with the body, the manner in which he or she takes responsibility for it, and even the meaning given to one's very existence. Yet, in the eyes of the Fathers, even the most commonplace and ordinary patterns of eating behavior are revelatory for our relationships with the world, with God, and thereby with ourselves. It is for this reason that they advise us to fight against *gastrimargia*—the passion of gluttony (trivialized in the West as greediness, or even the love of good food)—which consists in becoming attached to different kinds of food and in seeking them out, whether quantitatively or qualitatively, not with the aim of getting something to eat and maintaining one's health, but simply on account of the pleasure they are able to give. It is a passion that seems to the Fathers to be not just a veritable perversion of the nutritive function, but also one of the main forms of pathological attachment to one's own body and to sensible reality. It is an attitude that seems to them to be basically idolatrous, since to those who give themselves up to it one may apply the words of St Paul: "[their] god is their belly" (Phil 3.19).[25] They make their sense of smell, their sense of taste, and indeed their entire digestive system the center of their being, and in a certain sense reduce themselves to this. Moreover, they turn food into an object of major, indeed essential, concern; their attention, their every thought and desire is

[25]See Gregory Palamas, *The Triads* 2.3.6.

focused on food, with the result that they become oblivious of all spiritual good.

Of course, food in itself is not contemptible for, as Christ says, "it is not what goes into the mouth [that] defiles a man" (Mt 15.11). Again, in the words of St Paul, "everything created by God is good, and nothing is to be refused, if it is received with thanksgiving" (1 Tim 4.4). But the dual purpose of nutrition should be respected: first, the natural objective of maintaining the health and strength of the body; second, on the spiritual level, a reason for giving thanks to the Creator, as St Paul points out in the above verse. Elsewhere he advises as follows: "whether you eat or drink ... do all to the glory of God" (1 Cor 10.31). Christ himself sets an example for us, when he gives thanks to his Father before distributing food to those around him (cf. Mt 15.36; Mk 8.6; Jn 6.11, 13). In doing likewise, we regain the attitude of Adam and Eve in their prelapsarian state, as they contemplated God through his creatures and made eucharistic use of what he had given them. Just as the eating of the fruit of the tree of the knowledge of good and evil seemed to certain Fathers a good symbol of ancestral sin, even so the eucharistic consumption of food is correlatively a particularly appropriate way of representing a relationship between humans and the world in which the world is no longer an end in itself, is no longer closed in on itself, no longer separates us from God, and hence no longer diverts us from our spiritual vocation and destiny. Instead, it has again become transparent to the divine energies, constituting a means of access to God and of union with him.

As with our eating behavior, so with our sexual behavior. The Fathers do not see this as a trifling matter, since basic spiritual values are involved that are connected in particular with the value we put on our body, and in a wider sense on our own person and that of other people, and that also have a bearing on our relationship with God.

We have seen that, according to the Fathers, the use of sexuality is by no means an original characteristic of human nature. It only appeared as a consequence of the sin of our first parents, as a providential means of enabling the human race to perpetuate itself. For this reason, following St Paul (cf. Heb 13.4; 1 Cor 7.28), they recognize its complete legitimacy within the framework of marriage and even proclaim its value,[26] deeming it to have been originally blessed by God and to be called to the same sanctification as every other function of human nature.

Thus, within marriage, the sexual passions (referred to as *porneia* in Greek) that a Christian must struggle with and overcome consist not in using the sexual function, but in doing so in a way that is perverse or improper; that is to say, in a manner contrary to its natural purpose.[27] There is abuse—or, more exactly, a bad use—when one engages in sexual activity simply with a view to the pleasure to be derived from it, when pleasure becomes the sole aim.[28] Such an aim is perverse and pathological for several reasons.

To begin with, it negates one of the principal purposes of sexuality, the most obvious and the one that is inherent in its very nature: namely, procreation.[29]

Yet, however fundamental this may be, the Fathers do not see it as the only purpose,[30] nor even the most important.[31] Procreation in the human species might well be looked upon as the natural result of

[26] See, for example, Gregory of Nyssa, *On Virginity* 7. Gregory of Nazianzus, *Oration* 37.9. John Chrysostom, *On Virginity* 8, 9, 10, 25; *Six Homilies on Isaiah 6*, 3.3; *Homilies on Genesis* 21.4; *First Homily on Marriage* 1.2. The first canon of the Council of Gangra (fourth century) stipulates that anyone who "condemns marriage" or conjugal relationships should be anathema.

[27] See Maximus the Confessor, *Centuries on Love* 3.4.

[28] See ibid. 2.17.

[29] See Clement of Alexandria, *The Instructor* 2.10; *The Stromata* 2.23; 3.11.72. Basil of Ancyra, *On the True Purity of Virginity* 38. Dorotheos of Gaza, *Discourses and Sayings* 15. John Chrysostom, *Homilies on the Gospel of St Matthew* 27.1; *First Homily on Marriage* 1.3; *On Virginity* 19. Isaac the Syrian, *Ascetical Homilies* 27. Maximus the Confessor, *Centuries on Love* 2.17.

[30] See Basil of Ancyra, *On the True Purity of Virginity* 38. Basil of Caesarea, *Homily on the Martyr Julitta* 5; *On the Renunciation of the World* 2. John Chrysostom, *On Virginity* 9, 19, 25, 26, 34; *Six Homilies on Isaiah 6*, 3.3; *Homilies on Genesis* 21.4; *First Homily on Marriage* 1.2–3; *On Choosing a Wife* 3.5.

[31] See John Chrysostom, *First Homily on Marriage* 1.3; *On Virginity* 19. It is worth noting that not a single New Testament reference to marriage mentions procreation as its purpose or justification.

the sexual union rather than its actual aim.[32] The sexual act is in the first place one of the ways in which a man and a woman are united; it is one of the ways in which their mutual love is manifested, being an expression of this love on a particular level of their being—that of the body.[33] The prime purpose of the sexual union is love, as well as the spiritual benefits to be obtained from such a union within marriage, along with the other modes of conjugal union.[34] However, it must be made clear that from a Christian point of view conjugal love is seen as the union of two *persons*; that is, of two beings conceived in their fullness of spirit, soul, and body, in their spiritual dimension, and their uniqueness. It is a union that is fulfilled in Christ with a view to the kingdom, being sealed both as to its nature and purpose by the grace of the Holy Spirit that is conferred by the sacrament of marriage. This understanding of the sacrament subordinates the sexual union, and all other forms of union between the spouses, to the spiritual dimension of their being and their love.[35] Thus the sexual union must be preceded ontologically not just by an affective union, but by the spiritual union which gives it its meaning and value. It is within such a framework alone that its purpose—as well as that of the finality of the nature of the persons who are brought into relation with one another—can be respected.[36]

When sexual unions takes place outside any spiritual context and with the sole intention of seeking sensual pleasure, this inevitably has a damaging effect, profoundly distorting the normal pattern of one's relationship with God, self, and neighbor.

In the first place, the exclusive desire for sexual pleasure that characterizes the sexual passion exploits the appetitive power,

---

[32]This is implicit in the wording of the prayers said by the priest during an Orthodox Wedding Service. See F. Mercier, *La Prière des Églises de rite byzantin* (Chevetogne: Monastère de Chevetogne, 2nd ed.,1948), vol. 1, 405.

[33]See Basil of Ancyra, *On the True Purity of Virginity* 38.

[34]See Basil of Ancyra, ibid. Basil of Caesarea, *Homily on the Martyr Julitta* 5; *On the Renunciation of the World* 2. John Chrysostom, *On Virginity* 9, 19, 25, 26, 34; *Six Homilies on Isaiah 6*, 3.3; *Homilies on Genesis* 21.4; *First Homily on Marriage* 1.2–3; *On Choosing a Wife* 3.5.

[35]See Basil of Ancyra, *On the True Purity of Virginity* 38.

[36]See ibid.

diverting it away from God who should be its basic goal. Obsessed by the sensual enjoyment this passion gives, the human being deprives himself of spiritual blessings. It is clear that the sexual passion, like all other passions, brings about a reversal of values at the highest level. In general, in the life of the person concerned it puts the flesh before the spirit,[37] and sensual pleasure in the place of God. In fact, in its normal use—i.e., when sanctified by the sacrament of marriage, integrated and spiritually transformed by the love of the spouses (which is spiritual, not merely affective)—the sexual union, like all other ways in which the married couple are united, is transparent to God and realizes analogically[38] on its own level the union of Christ with the Church (cf. Eph 5.20–32). In this way it acquires a mystical meaning (cf. Eph 5.32). In the sexual passion, on the contrary, it becomes an obstacle to encountering God. It ceases to be the expression on a certain level of a love that is rooted in the Spirit (and that is thus in a sense a spiritual act), becoming instead a purely carnal act, closed in on itself, autonomous, impenetrable to any form of transcendence. Pleasure as an end in itself becomes an absolute that excludes God and takes his place. Through the sexual passion we make of the pleasures of the flesh an idol, just as through gluttony we make an idol of food.

Second, and as a consequence, for people in the grip of this passion, the center of their being is no longer the image of God, but their own sexual function. In a way, they reduce themselves to this, just as those dominated by the passion of gluttony reduce themselves, as we have seen, to their gustatory and digestive functions. Thus they become decentered and are out of touch with their true self; they are alienated. In their case, the sexual function—since it is not subordinated to spiritual love, as it should be—reaches the point where it occupies an excessive, indeed exclusive, place (as is quite

[37]See Maximus the Confessor, *On the Lord's Prayer*.

[38]The analogy between sexual union and spiritual union is used copiously both in Scripture and in patristic writings. It is what inspires the *Song of Songs*, to take but one well known example.

visible with those commonly called "sex addicts") and replaces love with naked, impulsive desire.

In this way, as St Basil of Ancyra notes, the soul comes to lag behind the body.[39] The ordering of human faculties is thus drastically altered and a deep-seated imbalance is established in one's being. Intelligence, will, and affectivity all cease to be at the service of the spirit, cease to be informed and ordered by it, and are henceforth at the service of sexual desire in the pursuit of pleasure. Governed by his instincts alone, man is nothing more than an animal.[40]

The sexual passion causes many of the body's functions—the senses in the first place—to become diverted from their normal purpose, becoming instead means of sexual pleasure.[41] One can even say that this diverting affects the entire body. In asserting that "the body is not for sexual immorality" (1 Cor 6.13), St Paul clearly indicates that those who give themselves up to this passion are using the body in a way that is against nature and abnormal. If we reduce the body to being a mere instrument of sexual pleasure, we deny our spiritual dimension and transcendent destiny; we disregard the image of God in which we are created, and thus "forget [our] human nature."[42] We profane that which is by nature sacred and deiform, we "defile the temple of God,"[43] turning the temple of the Holy Spirit—a place of prayer—into a den of thieves. We make a prostitute (cf. 1 Cor 6) of someone who is called to be spiritually married to Christ both as a member of his Church as well as in human marriage, which is an icon of this.[44] Caught up in the sexual passion, such a person takes no heed of God's will regarding the use of the body (cf. 1 Thess 4.3–7); thus "he sins against his own body" (1 Cor 6.18) and "rejects . . . God" himself (1 Thess 4.8).

<hr />

[39]See Basil of Ancyra, *On the True Purity of Virginity* 38.

[40]See Gregory of Nyssa, *The Life of Moses* 2.302.

[41]See Mt 5.27. John Cassian, *The Institutes* 6.12. Basil of Ancyra, *On the True Purity of Virginity* 13. John Chrysostom, *Homilies on Matthew* 17.1.

[42]Gregory of Nyssa, *The Life of Moses* 302.

[43]1 Cor 3.17.

[44]See John Chrysostom, *Homilies on First Thessalonians* Homily 5.

Nevertheless, the above considerations regarding the body should not cause us to overlook the fact that it is not always involved in sexual passion, or at least that it is most often involved only in a secondary manner. Human sexuality is in the mind before it is in the body. And though it is true that in certain cases desire may be aroused in the soul as a result of bodily impulses, even in these cases the soul may be considered to retain the initiative insofar as it has at its disposal the power to allow these impulses to develop or, on the contrary, the power to refuse to let them do so. In any case, it must be stressed that one can succumb to the sexual passion in thought alone,[45] by the enjoyment of depictions, more specifically of images.[46] When these are not produced by the senses or the memory, they can be fabricated by the imagination under the pressure of urges and of desire.[47] This may even give rise to actual hallucinations.[48] In this way, the sexual passion makes those obsessed by it live in a world of phantoms and fantasy,[49] immersing them in an unreal universe.

Love is an opening up to another person, and a free gift of self. Each of the two people united by love gives his or her self to the other and receives the other in return. In this communion they are each enriched, blossoming to the full extent of their being, even into divine infinity if their love is nourished by grace, as it should be, and has the kingdom as its ultimate goal. Sexual passion, by contrast, is a form of *philautia*, revealing an egotistical love of self. It causes the person it possesses to be introverted, completely shutting out other people. It prevents all genuine exchange, since under its influence those affected are only concerned with their own interests. They give nothing to the other person, wishing only to receive, and taking only that which satisfies their passionate desire. Whatever they

[45] See, for example, *Apophthegmata Patrum* (The Anonymous Series) 46. Macarius of Egypt, *Homilies* as paraphrased by Symeon Metaphrastis 116. Nicetas Stethatos, *On the Inner Nature of Things and on the Purification of the Intellect* 17.

[46] See Maximus the Confesseur, *Centuries on Love* 3.53.

[47] See Evagrius Ponticus, *On the Eight Thoughts (Antirrheticus)* 2.21; *The Monk: A Treatise on the Practical Life* 8.

[48] See Evagrius Ponticus, *The Monk: A Treatise on the Practical Life* 8.

[49] See John Chrysostom, *Homilies on the Gospel of St Matthew* 17.2.

receive is thought of as the result of their own desire, rather than a gift from the other person. Impassioned people give themselves the other person, the other being nothing more than an intermediary between them and their self. Thus the sexual passion imprisons man within his self; more specifically and more restrictively, it imprisons him in the confined, closed world of his carnal sexuality, his instincts, his urges, and his fantasies, shutting him off completely from the boundless worlds of love and spirit.

Third, when the sexual passion takes the form of enjoying an imaginary representation of the other, this other ceases to exist as a person or fellow being and becomes a mere object of fantasy, created by the projection of the desires of the impassioned person. However, it is not only a prior imaginary conception of others that can distort one's view of them as they are in reality. For when this passion is activated at the expense of a concrete person who is actually present, it likewise brings about a diminishing of this person. To someone in the grip of the sexual passion, others are neither appreciated as persons nor perceived as having a spiritual dimension; their basic reality as creatures made in the image of God is ignored. They are reduced to that aspect of their external appearance which is likely to satisfy the impassioned person's desire for pleasure. They become, in the eyes of such a person, a mere instrument of pleasure, an object. In some cases, their inner being is denied altogether, along with the entire dimension that transcends the sexual level; in particular their conscience, their higher emotional life, and their will. Moreover, impassioned people brush aside the freedom of the other, being concerned only with the satisfaction of their own desire, which most often seems to them to be an absolute necessity, one that pays no attention to the desire of the other person. As a consequence of all this, others are no longer recognized or respected in their otherness or for the uniqueness of their personal reality, since these qualities only reveal themselves when we can freely express ourselves and are thus able to manifest the higher spheres of our being. Reduced by sexual passion to the generic, animal dimension of carnal sexuality, human beings become practically interchangeable, like so many objects.

Thus it transpires that those under the influence of the sexual passion see their neighbors as they are not; they do not see them as they are. In other words, they acquire a distorted vision of those with whom their passion brings them into contact. Thereafter all relationships between them become totally perverted.

The virtue that is the opposite of the sexual passion is chastity, in the strict sense of the term. Two areas can be distinguished: chastity in the context of monasticism, celibacy, and the widowed state; and chastity within the context of marriage itself.

We should first remind ourselves that, from the Christian point of view, sexual activity can only have meaning and can be practiced in a healthy, normal fashion only within the context of conjugal love. This is why it is excluded a priori from celibacy and the monastic life. In addition, the virtue of chastity—in the narrow sense—presupposes and denotes, in this latter context, a total abstinence from any sexual act and above all from any sexual desire. This in turn presupposes perfect continence and restraint; that is, the ability to control and suppress completely all sexual urges and desires.

Inasmuch as sexuality is connected with the reproduction of the species, it is a particularly powerful instinct, firmly rooted in humanity's present nature. This makes total abstinence especially difficult to achieve and explains the length and difficulty of the combat that must be undertaken.

Because the sexual passion is one that the body is instrumental in arousing and realizing, its therapy "especially requires bodily abstinence as well as spiritual care of the soul."[50] Thus fasts,[51] vigils,[52] exhausting work,[53] and the other classic forms of asceticism

[50]John Cassian, *The Conferences* 5.4. Cf. John of Gaza, *Letter* 248.

[51]See John Cassian, *The Institutes* 6.1–2; *The Conferences* 5.4, 7.2, 12.4, 5, 15. John Climacus, *The Ladder* Step 15.12, p. 172; Step 19, p. 195. Maximus the Confessor, *Centuries on Love* 1.45; 2.19; 3.13. *Apophthegmata Patrum* (The Anonymous Series) 51. *Ethiopic Collectio Monastica* 13.33. Evagrius Ponticus, *The Monk: A Treatise on the Practical Life* 17. Barsanuphius, *Letter* 255.

[52]See *Apophthegmata Patrum* (The Anonymous Series) 51. John Cassian, *The Conferences* 5.4, 7.2, 12.4, 5, 15. John Climacus, *The Ladder* Step 15.12, p. 172; Step 19.4, p. 195. Maximus the Confessor, *Centuries on Love* 1.45, 2.19, 3.13.

[53]See *Apophthegmata Patrum* (The Anonymous Series) 36. John Cassian, *The*

that mortify the body are essential in order to face temptation, to be continent, to preserve abstinence, and to conquer the sexual passion at the bodily level.

Nevertheless, although such methods supply precious and often indispensable assistance, they are by no means sufficient to enable us to overcome this passion. The main reason for this is that the seat of the sexual function lies not in the body alone, but also in the soul. As we have said, human sexuality is as much in the mind as in the body, if not more so. Thus it is also necessary to fight the sexual passion on the level of the soul as much as, if not more than, on the level of the body. All the Fathers insist that chastity does not consist simply or principally in bodily continence[54] and that this in itself is useless, if the soul remains preoccupied by impure desires and imaginings. This is because "desire does not come from the body, even though it expresses itself through the body."[55] The principle of chastity is essentially in the soul and consists primarily in "integrity or purity of heart."[56] Since desires, impassioned thoughts, imaginings, and fantasies originate in the heart (cf. Mt 15.19), the main method for curing the sexual passion consists in "guarding the heart."[57] Requiring spiritual discernment and vigilance, this consists in rejecting impure thoughts, memories, and imaginings as soon as they arise, whilst they are still only suggestions, so as to avoid consenting to them and taking pleasure in them, and thus making room for the passion in the heart and thence in the body.[58]

To guarding the heart must of course be added prayer: prayer of the mind and of the heart, but also of the body, as manifested in

Conferences 5.4, 12.4, 5; The Institutes 5.10, 6.1. John Climacus, The Ladder Step 15.12, p. 172. Maximus the Confessor, Centuries on Love 2.19, 3.13.

[54]See, for example, Apophthegmata Patrum (The Anonymous Series) 46. John Cassian, The Institutes 6.4; The Conferences 13.5, 12.10–11.

[55]Clement of Alexandria, The Stromata 3.4.34.

[56]See John Cassian, The Institutes 6.19. John Climacus, The Ladder Step 15.8, p. 172.

[57]See John Cassian, The Institutes 6.2.

[58]See Apophthegmata Patrum (The Anonymous Series) 31, 33, 46, 52, 53. John Cassian, The Institutes 6.9. Barsanuphius, Letters 86, 248, 256. John of Gaza, Letter 180. John Climacus, The Ladder Step 15.6, p. 172.

such gestures as making the sign of the cross, bows, as well as small and great prostrations (*metanias*) such as are commonly practiced in the Orthodox Church. For by our own strength and without God's help, we shall never manage to conquer a passion that is all the more powerful for being fueled by an instinct deeply rooted in our nature and directly connected with the vital instincts, the instinct for self-preservation.

Monastic total abstinence takes on its full meaning in the context of the rationale and ultimate aim of monasticism, which is the complete consecration of oneself to God. The monk refrains from marrying so that he may have no other care than God, so that he may be able to consecrate to him alone all his desire, all his love, all his intelligence, and all his strength. This is far more difficult within the framework of marriage, as St Paul observes (1 Cor 7.32–35). By chastity and total abstinence, a monk recovers the state human nature had in paradise,[59] a state that assimilates him to the condition of the angels[60] and prefigures life in heaven,[61] according to the words of Christ himself: "For in the resurrection they neither marry nor are given in marriage, but are like angels of God in heaven" (Mt 22.30). Which is why, in the eyes of the Fathers, the monastic state is unquestionably superior to that of marriage, and of the two seems the more perfect.

This does not mean, however, that Christianity condemns or despises marriage (as has already been noted). At the same time as praising the pre-eminence of virginity and monastic celibacy, the Fathers also celebrate the value of marriage—an institution that Christ himself sanctified, moreover, by his presence at the wedding in Cana and by performing there the first miracle in his public life. It is noteworthy that the majority of patristic texts praising virginity also contain a simultaneous apology for marriage.

---

[59]See Gregory of Nyssa, *On Virginity* 12.

[60]See Basil of Caesarea, *Letter* 46.2. Gregory of Nyssa, *On Virginity* 2, 4. Basil of Ancyra, *On the True Purity of Virginity* 51. John Chrysostom, *On Virginity* 11–12.

[61]See Origen, *Fragments on Romans* 29.

In marriage, chastity still has meaning and even constitutes a virtue that should be cultivated. But its precise nature is somewhat different in marriage from what it is for a celibate, a monk or nun. Whereas in celibacy the presumption is that abstinence will be total, within the framework of a Christian marriage—on account of its strictly monogamous character—such total abstinence is required only with regard to extra-conjugal sexuality. (It goes without saying that every form of sexual perversity, such as homosexuality, is a priori excluded.)[62]

The "conjugal chastity" referred to by the Fathers—echoing the advice of St Paul that "marriage is honorable among all, and the bed undefiled" (Heb 13.4)—does not imply an abstention from all sexual activity. Sexual intercourse is an essential part of marriage. The Apostle makes things sufficiently clear when he writes elsewhere, "Let the husband render to his wife the affection due to her, and likewise also the wife to her husband. The wife does not have authority over her own body, but the husband does. And likewise the husband does not have authority over his own body, but the wife does. Do not deprive one another except with consent for a time, that you may give yourselves to fasting and prayer; but then come together again . . ." (1 Cor 7.3–5). This teaching of St Paul shows that abstinence does have a place within the very framework of married life, though for a limited time only and in connection with specific spiritual requirements. St Gregory of Nyssa even goes so far as to write that "whoever practices [continence] to excess has a sick conscience, as the Apostle says" (1 Tim 4.2), since he "is despising marriage."[63]

There is such a thing as a chaste sexual union. As St Clement of Alexandria writes, it is possible for spouses to come together "without

---

[62]Homosexuality and other forms of sexual perversion are quite clearly condemned by Scripture, as well as by the Fathers. See in particular Lev 18.22–24; 20.13–17; Rom 1.26–27.1; Cor 6.9; 1 Tim 1.10.

[63]Gregory of Nyssa, *The Life of Moses* 289. [The above translation reflects the vocabulary of Larchet's quotation from the French edition rather than that found in published English versions.—Trans.] See also *On Virginity* 7.

betraying in their union the rules of chastity."[64] Concerning those who denigrate sexual intercourse, he even goes so far as to declare as follows: "[Some] people say that sexual intercourse is polluted. Yet they owe their existence to sexual intercourse! Must they not be polluted?"[65] He further points out that sexual activity is sanctified by marriage and a spiritual life: "Personally, I think that the seed coming from consecrated people is sacred too. So it is not just our spirit which ought to be consecrated. It is our character, our life, our body."[66]

The Fathers frequently stress the fact that sexuality is not evil in itself, but that everything depends on the way it is practiced. As St Methodius of Olympus notes, "Nothing is to be considered as evil in itself, but becomes so by the act of those who used it in such a way; for when properly and purely made use of, it comes out pure, but if disgracefully and improperly, then it becomes disgraceful."[67]

In our analysis of the sexual passion, we have seen that what characterizes it is an abuse of the sexual function, consisting in its use with a view to sensual gratification. This amounts to a perversion of its function in the sense that, by its very nature, it is intended for procreation; but also and more fundamentally, as we have said, it is intended to be one of the manifestations of the love the spouses have for each other, dependent on the other forms of their union, notably its spiritual dimension. Thus, the elimination of the sexual passion and the acquisition of chastity in marriage must consist above all in a restoring of sexuality's natural and normal purpose.

The first principle is that the married couple should not come together simply in order to obtain sensual pleasure; in other words, they should not make pleasure the aim and object of their union.[68] They should take care not to be dominated by pleasure,[69] not to

---

[64]Clement of Alexandria, *The Stromata* 3.6. [See the comment inserted in the previous note.—Trans.]

[65]Ibid. 3.6.

[66]Ibid. 3.6.46–47.

[67]Methodius of Olympus, *The Banquet of the Ten Virgins* 2.5. See also Dorotheos of Gaza, *Discourses* 15.162.

[68]See Dorotheos of Gaza, ibid. Maximus the Confessor, *Centuries on Love* 2.17.

[69]See Gregory of Nyssa, *On Virginity* 7.

become attached to it, not even to seek it out, and eventually no lon-ger to be attracted by it.[70] This does not mean the refusal or exclusion of the pleasure that is naturally connected with sexual intercourse, but simply a certain detachment towards it, the refusal to make of it an absolute. Pleasure should be the consequence of their union, something that is given in addition.

Any sexual union should in fact take place within the framework of the mutual love of the spouses, and should bring about on the level of their bodies a union analogous to that which takes place between them on the level of their souls and so enables their com-plete union, causing them to become, in the words of Scripture, "one flesh," at the same time as one soul and one spirit. Chastity within marriage presupposes that this bodily union constitutes neither an absolute nor an end in itself (that is, an autonomous act) but is perfectly integrated into and subordinated to the mental union of the couple—both affective and intellectual—and even more so their spiritual union. St Basil of Ancyra writes as follows: "When the reason, which is in the soul, has souls under its control and forms relationships between them for that which is clearly essential, it is natural that their union be accompanied by the lawful union of the bodies in which [these souls] reside. However, when souls propose to one another something other in the first place and when the bod-ies, in search of pleasure and—being so absorbed in what they are doing—join together the souls that are in them so as to put them at the service of the passion that excites them, the fact that the souls are dragged along in the wake of the vices of the flesh renders such a sexual union unlawful."[71]

Conjugal chastity also presupposes that the spouses are not dominated by desire or sexual urges, and that their union is not determined by them. Clement of Alexandria sets forth this prin-ciple: "we should never act from desire."[72] What should preside over their union is not instinct, which is an impersonal manifestation of

[70]See John Cassian, *The Conferences* 12.10.
[71]Basil of Ancyra, *On the True Purity of Virginity* 38.
[72]Clement of Alexandria, *The Stromata* 3.6.58.

our biological nature; nor a mere urge, which is the expression of this; nor even desire, but love—not simply in its mental, psychological dimension, but spiritual as well. In this sense, conjugal chastity presupposes a certain continence, a degree of self-restraint that allows one to curb instinctive movements, to moderate one's desire, to control one's urges, and to abstain from every thought or imagining that might be connected with them. This is why St Gregory of Nyssa advises that one should use one's sexuality with moderation,[73] "sparingly . . . and [with] restraint."[74] It is why St Gregory of Nazianzus stresses the need for a well-balanced approach, so as to avoid giving too much space to the flesh.[75] This is indispensable if the union is not to be a mere means of satisfying desire, and if the person and freedom of the spouse is to be respected. Yet it is also necessary if one is to avoid becoming "nothing but flesh and blood"[76] and ceasing to give priority in one's life, and in married life itself, to the spiritual.[77] As St Gregory of Nyssa notes, "There is no small danger for [man] lest, cajoled in the valuation of pleasure, he should think that there exists no other good but that which is enjoyed along with some sensual emotion, and, turning altogether from the love of immaterial delights, should become entirely of the flesh, seeking always his pleasure only there, so that his character will be a Pleasure-lover, not a God-lover" (2 Tim 3.4).[78] Particularly formidable is the strength of the habit that attaches man to the pleasures of the flesh, as St Gregory also points out when referring to the example of many people who "make within themselves a broad path for passion; so that the stream of their love leaves dry the abandoned channel of the higher way and flows abroad in indulgence."[79] Which is why he gives the following precept: "Our view of marriage is this; that the pursuit of heavenly things should be one's first care, but that

[73]See Gregory of Nyssa, *On Virginity* 7.
[74]Ibid. 8.
[75]See Gregory of Nazianzus, *Oration* 37.9.
[76]Gregory of Nyssa, *On Virginity* 8.
[77]See ibid. 8
[78]Ibid. 8.
[79]Ibid. 9.

one should not despise marriage, if one can use its advantages with sobriety and moderation."[80]

Typically, the effect of the sexual passion is to separate us from God. Chastity, on the contrary, aims to reunite us with him, and does—so much so that St John Climacus says that it "makes us as familiar with God . . . as any man may be."[81] Whereas in the sexual passion desire loses interest in God and spiritual reality, becoming absorbed in carnal reality in order to seek out sensual pleasure, one of the main objectives of continence and chastity is to enable desire to recover its normal, natural commitment to God. For, in fact, it cannot be committed to different things without becoming divided and thus having to deprive the one of what it gives to the other. Thus the chief role of continence and chastity in marriage is to establish an economy of desire, so that it does not become involved in sexuality to such a degree that it exhausts itself, thereafter ceasing to have spiritual reality as its main aim.[82]

This enables us to understand that the combat against the sexual passion and the acquisition of chastity consist, in effect, in a conversion of desire, so that spiritual love might take the place of carnal love. It is in this sense that we should understand St John Climacus' well-known assertion that "a chaste man is someone who has driven out bodily love by means of divine love, who has used heavenly fire to quench the fires of the flesh."[83]

Whereas, in married life, the sexual passion implies a love of the other outside God—a purely carnal love, closed in on itself and thus opaque to the divine energies—chastity, on the contrary, implies a love of the other in God and a love of God in the other. Chastity brings about a transfiguration of love, causes it rise to the spiritual plane, where it becomes entirely transparent to God. It imparts to it a mystical sense (cf. Eph 5.32), enabling it to realize analogically

[80]Ibid. 8–9. [The available English version has been modified to tally with the French edition.—Trans.]
[81]John Climacus, *The Ladder* Step 15.35, p. 176.
[82]See Gregory of Nyssa, *On Virginity* 8.
[83]John Climacus, *The Ladder* Step 15.2, p.171.

the mystery of Christ's love for the Church, as St Paul stresses in his Epistle to the Ephesians (the section that is appointed to be read at Orthodox weddings): "Husbands, love your wife, just as Christ also loved the Church" (Eph 5.25); "'A man shall leave his father and mother and be joined to his wife, and the two shall become one flesh.' This is a great mystery, but I speak concerning Christ and the Church" (Eph 5.31–32).

8. *The Body during Prayer.*

We have already referred to "bodily prayer"—that is, the gestures and postures made by the body during prayer. Amongst those familiar to Orthodox Christians are the following: making the sign of the cross; remaining in a kneeling position; standing immobile with arms by one's side; keeping the head and trunk bent over for a few seconds; making small bows after the sign of the cross; making small prostrations (i.e., bending the head and trunk forward, touching the ground with the right hand) or great prostrations (in which one kneels with both hands placed on the ground in front of one and then touches the ground with the forehead). These gestures show that the body is participating in prayer in concert with the soul, in the way appropriate to it and according to its specific nature.[84] But one can add that, during prayer in general, the body lends its own strength to the soul, adopting a suitable posture (which might simply be a matter of keeping absolutely still in moments of intense concentration), exercising its various faculties or on the contrary refraining from doing so (for example, by closing the senses to external impressions) in order to facilitate such concentration. Thus prayer can indeed be seen to be one of "those activities which are common to ... the soul and to the body."[85]

This is especially true of a prayer that is very widespread in the Christian East—made widely known in the West by the famous

[84]See ibid. 15.80–81.
[85]Gregory Palamas, *The Triads* 2.2.12, N. Gendle, trans., 51.

book *The Way of a Pilgrim*[86]—that is usually called the "Jesus prayer," or the "prayer of the heart." It consists in the continuous repetition of a short formula whose traditional form is "Lord Jesus Christ, Son of God, have mercy on me, a sinner." This may be accompanied by a psycho-somatic method that is based on centuries-old experience—some Fathers trace it back to the Apostles—but which was defined with maximum precision by the spiritual masters of the Hesychast movement in the thirteenth and fourteenth centuries. This "method"—the term is used by the Fathers—pursues three principal objectives: first, to involve the body in prayer and to enable it, like the soul, to receive the ensuing benefits; second, to promote continuity of prayer, enabling the believer the better to respond to the advice of Christ and St Paul, to "pray without ceasing" (Lk 21.36; 1 Thess 5.17); third, to stimulate concentration, contemplation, and attentiveness.

To concentrate one's mind to this end, according to Hesychast spirituality, necessitates having "the mind in the heart." In order to understand what this means, one must be aware that in the spiritual vocabulary of the Christian East the word "heart" signifies two realities: one spiritual, the other physical. On the one hand, it is used in its commonly accepted meaning, to refer to the physical organ. On the other hand, in keeping with the principal meaning given to it in the New Testament, the "heart" refers to the inner man,[87] the totality of the soul's powers,[88] more specifically their root.[89] It is the ontological center of man, his very interiority.

---

[86] *The Way of a Pilgrim*, R. M. French, trans. (London: SPCK, 1930). [In 1943 the same publisher issued an expanded volume, which contained a sequel—*The Pilgrim Continues His Way*—also translated by R. M. French. Nowadays these continue most often to be published together in one volume.—Trans.]

[87] See, for example, Gregory of Nyssa, *Homilies on the Beatitudes* 6.4. Isaac the Syrian, *Ascetical Homilies* 30. Theoliptos of Philadelphia, *On Inner Work in Christ and the Monastic Profession*. Nicodemos of the Holy Mountain, *Handbook of Spiritual Counsel* 10.

[88] See Symeon the New Theologian, *The Three Methods of Prayer* 73. Nicephorus the Monk, *On Watchfulness*.

[89] See Isaac the Syrian, *Ascetical Homilies* 83.

The Hesychast Fathers observed by experience that between the heart understood in the spiritual sense, and the physical heart—center of the body and principle of its life—there exists an analogical correspondence by virtue of the unity of soul and body in the human compound, which means that the former is based in the latter[90] and that what affects the one affects the other, even though the spiritual heart is by nature independent of the physical heart.

The mind is itself one of the organs of the spiritual heart,[91] the most important, so much so that it is sometimes called "heart" by metonymy—although the phrase "eye of the heart," which is also frequently used, is more appropriate. Though it is by nature immaterial and independent of the body, it too has its seat in the physical heart.[92]

However, ordinarily—and we have seen that this is a consequence of ancestral sin—the mind is separated from the heart. It disperses itself, scattering itself in thoughts outside the heart, and thereby outside itself. There is here no contradiction, for though the mind by its very nature has its seat in the heart, it normally[93] grows away from it as a consequence of one of its two activities (*energeia*), the one St Dionysius the Areopagite calls a movement "along a straight line"[94] and which corresponds to the exercise of the reason, whose organ is the brain.[95] On the other hand, in the second of its activities—that Dionysius calls "circular" and that is "the most excellent and most appropriate"[96]—it does not spread itself abroad, but

[90]See Gregory Palamas, *The Triads* 1.2.3. Nicephorus the Monk, *On Watchfulness*. Nicodemos of the Holy Mountain, *Handbook of Spiritual Counsel* 10.

[91]See Isaac the Syrian, *Ascetical Homilies* 83.

[92]See Gregory Palamas, *The Triads* 1.2.3; 2.2, 27–30. Gregory notes that the union of mind and body—and thus of the heart—is experienced as a fact, though it is difficult to explain in conceptual terms.

[93]See Gregory Palamas, *The Triads* 1.2.3; 2.2.25–26.

[94]Dionysius the Areopagite, *On the Divine Names* 4.9, as quoted by Gregory Palamas, *The Triads* 1.2.5 in N. Gendle, trans., 44. See also Nicodemos of the Holy Mountain, *Handbook of Spiritual Counsel* 10.

[95]See Nicodemos, Ibid.

[96]Dionysius, Ibid, as quoted by Gregory Palamas, *The Triads* 1.2.5, in N.Gendle, trans., 44. See also Nicodemos, Ibid.

returns to itself,[97] is restored to itself,[98] remains united to the heart, and is thus kept safe from any deviation[99] or digression.

It is to this second activity of the mind that prayer should correspond. To be able to devote oneself to it exclusively, the first activity must cease. We must in other words "gather together our mind ... and lead it back again into the interior,"[100] in other words to bring the mind back into the heart and keep it there.

Basing their approach on the bond that, as we have seen, unites the physical and the spiritual hearts, the Hesychast Fathers advocate the psycho-somatic method as one that should enable the practitioner more easily to succeed in "keep[ing] his incorporeal self shut up in the house of the body," as St John Climacus puts it.[101]

We have given a detailed exposition of this method elsewhere, and demonstrated the deep-seated reasons with which the Hesychast Fathers justify it.[102] Let us simply recall here that it consists first, with head bent forward and chin resting on the breast,[103] in fixing one's gaze, though with eyes closed, on the "place of the heart";[104] second, in slowing down the rate of breathing, retaining the breath a little "so as not to breathe easily";[105] third, in uniting the mind with the breath and in making it enter into the chest along with the breath, down to the "place of the heart."[106]

As well as promoting concentration, vigilance, and attentiveness, this method enables one to establish continuity in prayer (even

[97]Dionysius, Ibid.

[98]See Basil of Caesarea, *Letter* 1. Theoliptos of Philadelphia, *Texts* 1. Callistus and Ignatius Xanthopoulos, *Directions to Hesychasts in One Hundred Chapters* 19. Nicodemos of the Holy Mountain, *Handbook of Spiritual Counsel* 10.

[99]See Dionysius, Ibid. Gregory Palamas, *The Triads* 1.2.5. Nicephorus the Monk, *On Watchfulness.*

[100]Gregory Palamas, *The Triads* 1.2.3 in *The Triads*, N.Gendle, trans., 43.

[101]John Climacus, *The Ladder* Step 27.7, p. 262.

[102]See our *Therapy of Spiritual Illnesses*, vol. 2, Part Three, ch. 3 (b).

[103]See Nicodemos of the Holy Mountain, *Handbook of Spiritual Counsel* 10.

[104]Symeon the New Theologian, *The Three Methods of Prayer* 72

[105]Ibid. See also Gregory of Sinai, *On Stillness.*

[106]See Callistus and Ignatius Xanthopoulos, *Directions to Hesychasts in One Hundred Chapters* 20, 23.

during sleep) by linking it to one's respiratory rhythm and thus in making it, as it were, the "breathing of the soul."

But, since the respiratory rhythm is involved—and hence the cardiac rhythm—it is a method that is not without risks and for that reason should be practiced only under the guidance of an experienced spiritual father. When practiced correctly, it has beneficial effects not just on the soul but also on the body, which it pacifies and thoroughly attunes.

On account of the importance it gives to the body, its highly developed character, and certain of its effects on both psyche and body, this method has sometimes been compared to yoga and has even been thought of as a "Christian yoga." In yoga, however, the method is a technique pure and simple that, like all techniques, necessarily achieves its objective. Moreover, in yoga the technique is the most important thing. The psycho-somatic method associated with Hesychastic prayer, on the other hand, plays only an auxiliary role.[107] In prayer no method can be thought of as a technique able in and of itself to produce spiritual effects, which can only be the fruit of divine grace, a free gift from God. What matters most in order to receive this grace is faith, zeal, and all the other virtuous dispositions that we manifest to God during prayer. The "Jesus prayer" or "prayer of the heart" is meaningful and of value only when it is closely linked to one's spiritual life as a whole. It must be accompanied by attentiveness, vigilance, and also by the three virtues to which the Fathers attribute an indispensable role: repentance,[108] humility,[109] and love of God.[110] It also requires one to be simultaneously engaged in combat against the passions (until one achieves

[107]See Ibid. 24.

[108]See, among others, Theoliptos of Philadelphia, *On Inner Work in Christ*. Callistus and Ignatius Xanthopoulos, *Directions to Hesychasts in One Hundred Chapters* 25, 80, 81.

[109]See, among others, Theoliptos of Philadelphia, *On Inner Work in Christ*. Callistus and Ignatius Xanthopoulos, *Directions to Hesychasts in One Hundred Chapters* 25, 45.

[110]See Theoliptos of Philadelphia, *On Inner Work in Christ*. Nicodemos of the Holy Mountain, *Handbook of Spiritual Counsel* 10.

impassibility;[111] that is, their extinction) and correlatively to be practicing the Christian virtues.[112] In other words, it is inseparable from an active keeping of all the divine commandments,[113] and likewise from liturgical and sacramental life within the Church.

It is nonetheless true that, if the above method is placed within its proper context and constraints, it fully restores the body to the place in the spiritual life that it should have. It offers to the mind and body—separated by sin and its consequences—the possibility of recovering to the utmost their profound spiritual unity, and above all of achieving the ultimate purpose of this unity, which is to give man the possibility of praising God and of being united with him with *all* his being, and so to realize Christ's first commandment: "Thou shalt love the Lord thy God with all thy heart, and with all thy soul, and with all thy mind, and with all thy strength" (Mk 12.30; Lk 10.27).

9. *The Body in Liturgical Life.*

Those who attend an Orthodox service for the first time are struck by the frequency with which the faithful use their body to participate in the prayers, in sharp contrast with the immobile posture to be seen in Western Christian places of worship.

The faithful repeatedly identify themselves with certain words sung by the priest, deacon or choir by making certain bodily movements. The most frequent of these is the sign of the cross—sometimes repeated three times and usually followed by a slight bow—though at certain moments of the services other gestures may be made by individual members of the congregation, such as the ones referred to and described previously. In particular, there is the small *metania* (in which the head and upper part of the body are bowed) and the great *metania* (which consists in kneeling then, with both hands on the floor, bowing forward until the forehead also touches the floor).

---

[111]See, for example, Symeon the New Theologian, *The Three Methods of Prayer* 72. Callistus and Ignatius Xanthopoulos, *Directions to Hesychasts in One Hundred Chapters* 86, 87.

[112]See Theoliptos of Philadelphia, *Texts* 3.

[113]See ibid. 5.

Sometimes the faithful keep their heads or trunks bowed, or kneel, for several moments at a time. Yet even when they stand erect and still, with arms by the side of the body, this too is a gesture of prayer. It is one so important and normal that Orthodox churches normally contain no chairs or benches. In fact, it is a posture that symbolizes the resurrection, that key point of the Christian faith and hope.[114]

In addition, mention may also be made of the "passive" liturgical participation of the body in the setting that is so characteristic of the Orthodox Church, where the splendor of the celebration, so often misunderstood by those who have no experience of its meaning, has an important spiritual role to play—the beauty of the architecture and the "decoration" of the churches whose walls are covered with frescoes and icons; the solemn character of the services; the richness of the celebrants' vestments; the magnificence of the chants; the incense; the lights of the lamps and candles; and so on. All these things—which never cease to awaken a sense of wonder in the faithful—have a fourfold meaning.

First, it is a question of praising God with means that—as far as is humanly possible—are worthy of his greatness and glory.

Second, it is a matter of offering to God that which we hold to be most beautiful, most precious—just as the Magi offered to Christ gold, frankincense, and myrrh.

Third, it is a question of symbolizing the kingdom of heaven. For example, St Germanus of Constantinople writes that "the church is an earthly heaven in which the supercelestial God dwells and walks about."[115] St Symeon of Thessalonica wrote in the same vein that

---

[114]The canons of the Orthodox Church proscribe kneeling on a Sunday, this being the day on which Christ's resurrection is celebrated. On this subject, see the fine study by Archimandrite Grigorios Papathomas, "Comment et pourquoi l'Église exclut l'agenouillement lorsqu'elle proclame la Résurrection et la vie du Siècle à venir selon la Tradition canonique de l'Église (Présentation sommaire des sources patristiques et canoniques)," in *Thysia Ainéseôs. Mélanges liturgiques offerts à la mémoire de l'Archevèque Georges Wagner* (1930–1993), (Paris: Presses Saint-Serge, 2005), 247–292.

[115]St Germanus, *On the Divine Liturgy* 1, P. Meyendorff, trans. (Crestwood, NY: St Vladimir's Seminary Press, 1985), 57.

"the shape of the divine temple also represents what is on earth, what is in heaven, and what is above the heavens."[116]

Last—and this is a point that we would wish to emphasize—it is about giving the faithful, in a symbolic way, a taste of the riches and glory of the kingdom of heaven, and also of the new conditions of existence there, when the body is transfigured along with all the senses. (We have already referred to the doctrine so dear to the Greek Fathers concerning the spiritual senses.)

The very interior of an Orthodox church introduces the body into a space that is different from the ordinary; it is a space transfigured and sacred, whose profound symbolism is superbly analyzed by St Maximus the Confessor in his *Mystagogia*.[117] He stresses in particular that the church's spatial structure symbolizes the human being: the altar representing the spirit, the sanctuary the soul, and the nave the body.[118] Conversely, the human being symbolizes the church: his spirit is, as it were, an altar; his soul, a sanctuary; and his body, a nave. And this not simply by their nature but by their own specific functions in spiritual life: the body represents in particular the practical or ethical dimension; the soul stands for the contemplative dimension; and the spirit its pinnacle, *theologia*, in which the believer receives from the Holy Spirit supernatural knowledge of the divine mysteries.[119]

As for liturgical time, by its cyclical character, by the intentionally repetitive nature of certain forms of prayer, and by the expansive nature of certain chants,[120] the souls and bodies of the faithful are admitted into another mode of time, close to eternity (and in any

---

[116]*The Liturgical Commentaries: St Symeon of Thessalonica*, S. Hawkes-Teeple, trans. (Toronto: Pontifical Institute of Mediaeval Studies, 2011), 91.

[117]See Maximus the Confessor, *Mystagogia* 2–5. See also our article, "La symbolique spirituelle de l'église selon la *Mystagogie* de Saint Maxime le Confesseur," in *L'Espace liturgique: ses éléments constitutifs et leur sens*. Conférences Saint-Serge. 52e Semaine d'études liturgiques (Rome: CLV-Edizioni liturgiche, 2006).

[118]See Maximus the Confessor, *Mystagogia* 4.

[119]See ibid. On the meaning of practice (*praxis*), contemplation (*theōria*) and theology (*theologia*) in Maximus, see our *Saint Maxime le Confesseur* (Paris: Les Éditions du Cerf, 2003), 175–185.

[120]This is particularly characteristic of Byzantine chant.

case symbolic of it), in which they neither grow weary nor become bored but rather have a feeling of well-being, experiencing what Peter was experiencing, when he said to Christ: "Lord, it is good for us to be here" (Mt 17.4).

Every aspect of the ecclesial environment contributes to the spiritual activation, elevation, and transfiguration of the senses: the frescoes, the icons, the flames of the hanging oil lamps, and the light of the candles all transfigure the sight; the chants, the hearing; the incense, the sense of smell; the oil (with which, during the Litya in Matins on feast days, the faithful are anointed), the sense of touch. By means of these images and symbols, the believers perceive, in proportion to the quality of their spiritual state, the first fruits of God's beauty, his light, his good odor (cf. 2 Cor 2.15), and his gentleness and sweetness, which will be revealed in their fullness in the kingdom of heaven.

Everything in the church is done so that the faithful may contribute, not only with their souls but also their bodies, to the glorification of God and so that, in exchange, their whole being may be transformed by his grace, for their salvation and deification.

CHAPTER FIVE

The Body Transfigured and Deified

1. *The Effects of Spiritual Life on the Body*

Spiritual life, which enables Christians to receive grace in their whole being (soul and body), has numerous positive effects on both. The body shares directly in the ordering, the unification, and the pacification that is established in the soul. This is particularly felt in prayer, especially the "prayer of the heart" that we referred to earlier. Insofar as they are united to God and assimilate the grace received from him, Christians share to a certain extent in the divine qualities. (As seen, the Fathers say that one has achieved the divine likeness, become "deified.")

When the soul participates in divine peace and the ordering brought about by grace, it communicates this to the body's functions; the divine beauty that is reflected in the soul is transmitted to the body, which in turn becomes radiant with it. The presence of the Holy Spirit—of whom St Irenaeus says he is "*iuvenescens*," that he makes young—marks the entire person. This is why many spiritual masters reach a grand old age whilst retaining astonishing physical vigor and a surprising youthfulness.[1] It is given to certain saints to manifest in their bodies the health they have found in their souls. "A man flooded with the love of God," writes St John Climacus, "reveals in his body, as if in a mirror, the splendor of his soul, a glory like that of Moses when he came face to face with God."[2] For some, this grace can become a source of health. "I suspect," continues St John Climacus, "that the bodies of these incorruptible men are immune

---

[1]See Callinicos, *Life of Hypatius* 26.4. Evagrius Ponticus, *Texts on Discrimination in respect of Passions and Thoughts* 10. ["Sickness is rare among us."—*Trans.*]

[2]John Climacus, *The Ladder* Step 30.17, p. 288.

to sickness, for their bodies have been sanctified and rendered incorruptible by the flame of chastity which has put out the flame [of the passions]."[3]

Those who live in intimacy with God are partly able to return to the condition of paradise: impassibility becomes attainable again in this world; incorruptibility and immortality are promised as future realities. The *Lives* of the saints show us in many ways that, when permeated with the divine energies, the body not only reveals its destiny—one that transcends the normal lot of matter—but to some extent is already exempt from the laws of nature, as is demonstrated by such diverse extraordinary phenomena as levitation, walking on water, the ability to see far-off things, bilocation, or surviving on no food other than Holy Communion. None of these manifestations has any value in itself, but they are signs that the other world, the kingdom of heaven, is a reality of which those who are worthy are granted an earnest here below, not only in their souls but their bodies.

2. *The Body Transfigured and Deified*

The radiance of the uncreated divine light manifested by certain saints because of the presence in them of the Holy Spirit,[4] is an experience analogous to the transfiguration of the Lord, both for such saints themselves as well as for those to whom it is granted to be witnesses. The saint manifests bodily the divine energies that have been received by grace but that, in his own case, Christ received from his divine nature. In this way, the saint bears witness to the deification that those found worthy will experience in its fullness after the general resurrection, but of which they receive an earnest even now as a gift from God in accordance with their level of spiritual

---

[3]John Climacus, *The Ladder* 30.19, p. 288.

[4]See, for example, *The Aim of Christian Life: The Conversation of St Seraphim of Sarov with N. A. Motovilov* by St Seraphim and N.A. Motovilov (Cambridge: Saints Alive Press, 2010). See also St Seraphim's conversation in I. Gorainov, *The Message of St Seraphim* (Oxford: SLG Press, 1973) or V. Zander, *St Seraphim of Sarov* (Crestwood, NY: St Validimir's Seminary Press, 1975).

perfection. St Maximus the Confessor strongly emphasizes that the body, along with the soul, is itself deified in its own way.[5] "The whole man," he writes, "is divinized by being made God by the grace of God who became man. He remains wholly man in soul and body by nature, and becomes wholly God in body and soul by grace and by the unparalleled divine radiance of blessed glory appropriate to him. Nothing can be imagined more splendid and lofty than this."[6]

3. *The Evidence of Relics*

Even in death the bodies of the saints reveal that, though still present in this world whilst awaiting the resurrection, they belong to the kingdom. They bear witness to the fact that the divine energies that permeated and transformed them remain present. Often their bodies undergo no corruption, are impervious to the putrefaction and dissolution that is the common lot, and instead remain intact, exhaling sweet perfumes. Through the divine energies that are still present in their relics,[7] the saints continue to work miracles, showing that God has allowed them to do so even in their new mode of existence. It is an existence in which the body is united to the soul in a different way, whilst remaining an integral part of the person. For this reason, the veneration of relics is not idolatry. It is not directed at an inanimate object, but concerns the persons[8] of whose bodies they remain a part, and through which these persons continue to express and manifest themselves, albeit in a different manner.

[5]See Maximus the Confessor, *Questions and Doubts* 142; *Ambigua* 20; *Questions to Thalassios* Prologue, 3, 6, 25, 33, 65.

[6]Maximus the Confessor, *Ambigua* 7.3 in *On the Cosmic Mystery of Jesus Christ: Selected Writings from St Maximus the Confessor*, P. M. Blowers and R. L. Wilken, trans. (Crestwood, NY: St Vladimir's Seminary Press, 2003), 63.

[7]See Gregory Palamas, *A New Testament Decalogue* 2.

[8]See the definition of faith given in 787 at the Seventh Ecumenical Council (Nicaea II), which rejected iconoclasm and rehabilitated the veneration not only of icons but also of relics. The veneration of relics—unknown in Protestantism and practically fallen into disuse in Catholicism—continues to have an important place in Orthodox piety, in the same way as icons.

4. *The Icon, Image of the Transfigured and Deified Body*

In an icon, saints are depicted in their divine-human reality—that of persons who remain human by nature but who have become god by grace. Their bodies seem to have retained all their human reality, but at the same time to have attained a superior mode of existence, divine in quality. Their solemn, hieratic appearance testifies to their entry into eternity and into the stability of the other world. The lightness of their clothing, which seems to defy the laws of gravity, is a sign that they themselves are no longer subject to the laws of physics. Their ascetic faces show them to be purified of all passion, liberated from all carnal heaviness, and henceforth free from all disharmony. The virtues—love, humility, compunction, gentleness, chastity, temperance, and so on—show through these faces, which seem simultaneously detached from the world and attached to God in an attitude of prayer and contemplation, whilst being at the same time open and present to those who look at them and venerate them. The divine energies, which primarily illumine their faces, seem to suffuse their entire bodies and to spread to all that surrounds them. The saints depicted seem indeed to have acquired by grace the divine likeness; radiantly they show forth the beauty of the image of God in which they were created.

It is important to note that the divine-human reality to which the saints have acceded by grace is manifested in and through their bodies. Here is further testimony to the fact that the body belongs to a person as one of the essential constituents of his or her being, that it exists in close union with the soul, that it fully participates in the spiritual life, and that it too is to be saved and deified. This transparency of the body to the divine energies shows that it is no longer in any way an obstacle to union with God, but shares fully in his life.

An icon bears witness to a world in which the body is no longer something purely external, dissociated from the subjective self. It no longer conceals the inner life, no longer misleads as to a person's true character, no longer constitutes an obstacle to meeting other people, and no longer poses a challenge by seeking to gain power over them.

In an icon the body seems to be in perfect union and harmony with the soul and the spirit, and seems able to give expression to them in unmediated fashion and without distortion. Moreover, because of the way in which the border is carved so that it stands proud, or is painted in such a way that it seems to do so, an icon has the appearance of a window that is open to the one looking at it. The use of inverse perspective reduces spatial depth and at the same time the distance between the person depicted and the spectator. As a result, an icon is not a closed world, shut in on itself, existing in and for itself, leaving the spectator outside and detached; rather, it reaches out to him, includes him, and makes him share in its spiritual reality. When we look at an icon, we do not feel judged by the person portrayed, we do not feel ourselves to be prisoners of his or her gaze. We experience no animosity but, on the contrary, feel we are respected, held in esteem, loved, and valued. Faced with this new, boundless world that is opened to us, we experience greater freedom and greater dignity. We feel that we are more intensely alive, and that there is more meaning and truth in our existence.

CHAPTER SIX

The Body, Dead and Resurrected

1. *The New Meaning of the Body's Tribulations*

The state in which the body will have become impassible, incorruptible, and immortal is a future reality, one which believers firmly hope to enjoy but of which here below they can obtain only an earnest—even if they be saints. *A fortiori* the same is true of deification. As we look forward to this state that will follow the resurrection, our body remains subject to the natural passions (to suffering, in particular), to corruption, and to death.[1]

But the meaning of suffering, corruption, and death has been fundamentally changed by Christ's saving economy. Previously they were means of alienation, domination, and destruction in the service of sin and the powers of evil; but he has made them into instruments that we can use for the purpose of our salvation.[2]

St Maximus the Confessor, in particular, shows how by his passion Christ radically altered the meaning of pain. Previously it was the consequence of sin and, as it were, a debt incurred to it by our nature; but by suffering unjustly—since he was without sin and was neither conceived nor born according to the ways in which the effects of ancestral sin are transmitted—he made of it a means by which we may condemn sin and gain access to divine life.[3]

Christ's victory over death means that for man death ceases to be the end; the separation of the body from the soul is no longer definitive, the body's dissolution no longer without a remedy. From

---

[1]We have analyzed the reasons for this in *The Theology of Illness*, 41–53.

[2]See ibid., 57–60. See also our *Dieu ne veut pas la souffrance des hommes*, 2nd ed. (Paris: Éditions du Cerf, 2008), chaps. 5–7.

[3]See Maximus the Confessor, *Questions to Thalassios* 61.

now on, as St John Chrysostom puts it, death is nothing more than the death of corruption[4] and the destruction of death.[5] Although we still must die, it is no longer so that we may cease to live, but so that—death having been transcended—we may live again, rise again, and put on incorruptibility and immortality.[6] For what is sown "is not made alive unless it dies" (1 Cor 15.36).

2. *The Body's Destiny after Death*

After death, the soul becomes detached from the body, which then suffers the same fate as the bodies of all other living creatures: it starts to rot, and its members disintegrate or dissolve according to their nature.

Nevertheless, although the body is detached from the soul, it is not separated from it. The soul remains in some way present in the body and maintains with it a close relationship.[7] As we have already noted, the body continues to belong to the person whose body it is,[8] and even to a certain extent continues to be this person. In this regard, it is significant that Christ himself—in the passage where Mary Magdalene pours perfume over his head—speaks of *his* burial, not that of his body: "in pouring this fragrant oil on my body, she did it for my burial" (Mt 26.12). Although dispersed, then, the dead body's constituent elements continue to have between them a certain relationship and a certain unity.

This explains the care with which a dead body is treated, notably in funeral rites.[9] It also justifies our spending a few moments in silence at the grave of a deceased person in the belief that it contains not just their body but that the soul too is present. It explains why we pray before their "remains" as to the total person. Finally, from

---

[4] See John Chrysostom, *Homily on the Resurrection of the Dead* 7; *Commentary on the Psalms* 48.5.
[5] See John Chrysostom, *Homilies on the Gospel of St Matthew* 34.4.
[6] See John Ambrose, *Death as a Good* 15.
[7] See Gregory of Nyssa, *On the Soul and the Resurrection* 59–62, 68.
[8] See ibid.
[9] See M. Andronikof, *Transplantation d'organes et éthique chrétienne*, 45–50.

the standpoint of Christian ethics, it rules out treating the body of a deceased person—whether the whole body or one or other of its organs—as an object. On the contrary, it implies that one should show it respect, the same respect that one owes to the deceased person.[10]

During the time following death, the body along with the soul awaits the resurrection.

3. *The Resurrected Body*

Through Christ (1 Thess 4.14), with him (ibid.), and in him (1 Cor 15.22), through the power of the Holy Spirit, God will indeed give life to the dead (Rom 8.11) and will resurrect their bodies. He will heal them from all their ills, according to the word of the prophet Isaiah: "The dead shall rise, and they that are in the tombs shall be raised, and they that are in the earth shall rejoice: for the dew from thee is healing to them" (Is 26.19). Then the body will be delivered from its past infirmities and will recover its wholeness. On this point, Tertullian writes: "If the flesh is to be repaired after its dissolution, much more will it be restored after some violent injury. . . . If we are changed for glory, how much more for integrity! Any loss sustained by our bodies is an accident to them, but their entirety is their natural property."[11]

After raising the body and wholly restoring it, God will make it incorruptible and immortal, "for this corruptible [body] must put on incorruption, and this mortal must put on immortality" (1 Cor 15.53). It is then that "we shall be changed" (1 Cor 15.52). But this does not mean that we shall put on a different body, other than the one we had on earth. It is neither a question of metempsychosis nor reincarnation. The Fathers insist on this.[12] We shall each put on

[10]See ibid.

[11]Tertullian, *On the Resurrection of the Flesh* 57.

[12]See, for example, John Chrysostom, *Homilies on 1 Corinthians* 41.1 and 42.2; *Homilies on 2 Corinthians* 10.2–3. Irenaeus of Lyons, *Against the Heresies* 5.2.3. Tertullian, *On the Resurrection* 52, 53, 55, 60, 62. Gregory of Nyssa, *On the Making of Man* 27–28; *On the Soul and the Resurrection* 59–62, 68.

again our own body, though it will be reconstructed, reconstituted, and will have attained another mode of existence—one that will be free from the imperfections, weaknesses, passibility, corruptibility, and the mortality that characterize its present nature. "So also is the resurrection of the dead. The body is sown in corruption, it is raised in incorruption. It is sown in dishonor, it is raised in glory. It is sown in weakness, it is raised in power" (1 Cor 15. 42–43). It will not live according to its present material mode of existence and so will not experience any kind of limitation, constraint, or restriction,[13] but it will be freed from the laws of nature as we now know them, just as is the body of Christ after his resurrection, to which our own bodies will have become similar.[14] Without ceasing to be a body, "it will become like the soul,"[15] from being a "natural body" it will become a "spiritual body" (1 Cor 15.44).[16] It will be perfectly united to the soul[17] and completely transparent to the spiritual energies.[18] In Christ's own words, after the resurrection we shall be "like the angels in heaven" (Mk 12.25; Mt 22.30; Lk 20.35–36).[19]

In this new condition in which it will no longer bear the image of "the man of dust" but of "the heavenly Man" (1 Cor 15.49), the body will no longer be subject to any form of corruption: it will no longer experience illness,[20] physical suffering,[21] or any kind of degeneration.[22]

We shall experience perfect bodily health, total and definitive, so that we shall be able to receive in body as in soul the fullness of grace

[13]See Gregory of Nyssa, *On the Deceased*, PG 46:532–36. Gregory Palamas, *The Triads* 1.3.36.

[14]See John Chrysostom, *Homilies on Philippians* 13.2.

[15]Maximus the Confessor, *Mystagogia* 7.

[16]See Gregory Palamas, *The Triads* 1.3.36.

[17]See Pseudo-Maximus the Confessor, *Scholia on the Divine Names*, PG 4:197.

[18]See Gregory Palamas, ibid.

[19]See ibid.

[20]See John Chrysostom, *Homilies on the Consolation of Death* 1.6. Ammonas *Letters* 1.2.

[21]See John Chrysostom, *Homilies on 2 Corinthians* 10.1–2; *Homilies on 1 Corinthians* 41.1. Ammonas, *Letters* 1.2.

[22]See Gregory of Nyssa, *On the Deceased*, PG 46:532–36; Tertullian, *On the Resurrection* 57.

and thus become, with our whole being, "partakers of the divine nature" (2 Pet 1.4) and able to enjoy for all eternity the divine blessings with all our bodily members and all the means that God gave us when, in the beginning, he created us so that we might "become gods." But now, by the power of the Holy Spirit who will transfigure and fill them with life, these means will be brought to perfection.

The human body will thereby achieve its ultimate destiny, which is to be deified along with the soul in the human person. It is this state that St Maximus is describing, when he writes that man "[will] remain wholly man in soul and body by nature, and become wholly God in body and soul by grace and by the unparalleled divine radiance of blessed glory appropriate to him."[23]

[23]Maximus the Confessor, *Ambigua* 7.3.

Bibliography

No bibliography is provided in the original. Below is a list of patristic texts (in English where available) that are frequently referred to in the footnotes by title alone.

Abbreviations:

ANF   *The Ante-Nicene Fathers*. Edited by Alexander Roberts and James Donaldson. 10 vols. Buffalo, 1885–1896. Reprint, Peabody, MA: Hendrickson, 1994. Available at *www.ccel.org*

NPNF   *The Nicene and Post-Nicene Fathers*. Series 1 and 2 (NPNF¹ and NPNF²). Edited by Philip Schaff. New York, 1886–1889. 28 vols. [14 vols. in each series]. Reprint, Peabody, MA: Hendrickson, 1994. Available at *www.ccel.org*

PG   Patrologia Graeca [= Patrologiae cursus completus: Series graeca]. Edited by J.-P. Migne. 162 vols. Paris, 1857–1866. Available at *www.documentacatholicaomnia.eu*

Ambrose. *Death as a Good (De bono mortis)*. PG 14:567ff. English translation in *Ambrose: Seven Exegetical Works*. Michael P. McHugh, trans. The Fathers of the Church Series, vol. 65. Washington, DC: Catholic University of America Press, 1972.

Ammonas. *Letters* in *The Letters of Ammonas*, Derwas Chitty, trans. Oxford: SLG Press. 1979.

Apophthegmata Patrum. *The Wisdom of the Desert Fathers: Apophthegmata Patrum* (The Anonymous Series), Benedicta Ward, trans. Oxford: SLG Press. 1975.

Athanasius of Alexandria. *Against the Heathen* in NPNF² 4.

_____. *On the Incarnation*, John Behr, trans. Pupular Patristics Series, vol. 44a. Crestwood, NY: St Vladimir's Seminary Press, 2011.

Athenagoras. *On the Resurrection of the Dead* in ANF 2.

Barsanuphius. *Letters* in *Barsanuphius and John: Letters*, Volume 1, John Chryssavgis, trans. Washington, DC: CUA Press, 2006. See also *Letters from the Desert: Barsanuphius and John, a Selection of Questions and Responses*. John Chryssavgis, trans. and ed. Popular Patristics Series, vol. 26. Crestwood, NY: St Vladimir's Seminary Press, 2003.

Basil of Ancyra. *On the True Purity of Virginity.* In French: *De la véritable intégrité dans la virginité*, C. Coudreau, trans. Ligugé: Abbaye Saint-Martin, 1981. Also in PG130:668–810 (attributed to Basil of Caesarea).

Basil of Caesarea. *Homily Explaining that God is Not the Cause of Evil* in *St Basil the Great: On the Human Condition*, Nonna Verna Harrison, trans. Popular Patristics Series, vol. 30. Crestwood, NY: St Vladimir's Seminary Press, 2005.

_____. *Letters* 1, 46, and 366 in NPNF^2 8.

_____. *Long Rules* and *On the Renunciation of the World* (i.e., *An Ascetical Discourse and Exhortation on the Renunciation of the World and Spiritual Perfection*) in *St Basil: Ascetical Works*, M. Monica Wagner, trans. Washington, DC: CUA Press, 1950.

_____. *On the Origin of Humanity* in *St Basil the Great: On the Human Condition*, Nonna Verna Harrison, trans. Popular Patristics Series, vol. 30. Crestwood, NY: St Vladimir's Seminary Press, 2005.

_____. *Homily on the Martyr Julitta* in *St Basil the Great on Fasting and Feasts*, Susan R. Holman and Mark DelCogliano, trans. Popular Patristics Series, vol. 50. Yonkers, NY: St Vladimir's Seminary Press, 2013.

Cabasilas, Nicholas. *The Life in Christ*, C. J. deCatanzaro, trans. Crestwood, NY: St Vladimir's Seminary Press, 1974.

Callistus and Ignatius Xanthopoulos. *Directions to Hesychasts* in *One Hundred Chapters* in *Writings from the Philokalia on the Prayer of the Heart*, E. Kadloubovsky and G. Palmer, trans. London: Faber and Faber, 1951.

Clement of Alexandria. *The Instructor* in ANF 2.

_____. *The Stromata* in ANF 2. For Book Three in English, see *lement of Alexandria: Stromateis, Books 1–3*, J. Ferguson, trans. Washington, CUA Press: 1991. This translation is also available at *www.earlychristianwritings.com*.

Cyril of Jerusalem. *Catechetical Lectures* in *Lectures on the Christian Sacraments*, Frank L. Cross, ed. Popular Patristics Series, vol. 2. Crestwood, NY: St Vladimir's Seminary Press, 1986.

Dionysius the Areopagite. *On the Divine Names* in *Pseudo-Dionysius: The Complete Works*, Colm Luibheid, trans. New York: Paulist Press, 1987.

Dorotheos of Gaza. *Discourses and Sayings*, E. Wheeler, trans. Kalamazoo, MI: Cistercian Publications, 1977.

Ethiopic Collectio Monastica. V. Arras, ed. Leuven: Peeters, 1963.

Evagrius Ponticus. *On Prayer* in *The Philokalia* vol. 1, G. E. H. Palmer, P. Sherrard & K. Ware, trans. London: Faber and Faber, 1979.

_____. *Maxims* in *Evagrius of Pontus: The Greek Ascetic Corpus*, R. E. Sinkewicz, trans. Oxford: OUP, 2003.

_____. *The Monk: A Treatise on the Practical Life* in ibid.

Gregory of Nazianzus. *Oration 37* in NPNF[2] 7.

Gregory of Nyssa. *Easter Sermons*, H. R. Drobner, trans. in *The Easter Sermons of Gregory of Nyssa*, A. Spira and C. Klock, eds. Cambridge, MA: Philadelphia Patristic Foundation, 1981.

_____. *Homilies on the Beatitudes*, S. G. Hall, trans. in *Gregory of Nyssa: Homilies on the Beatitudes*, Proceedings of the Eighth International Colloquium on Gregory of Nyssa, H. Drobner and H. Viciano, eds. Leiden: Brill, 2000.

_____. *Letter 3* (to Eustathia, Ambrosia, and Basilissa) in NPNF[2] 5 and *Gregory of Nyssa: The Letters*, Anna M. Silvas, trans. Leiden–Boston: Brill, 2007.

_____. *The Life of Moses*, A. J. Malherbe and E. Ferguson, trans. New York: Paulist Press, 1978.

_____. *On the Deceased* = *De mortuis* in PG 46: 497–537.

_____. *On the Making of Man* in NPNF² 5.

_____. *On the Soul and the Resurrection*, C. P. Roth, trans. Popular Patristics Series, vol. 12. Crestwood, NY: St Vladimir's Seminary Press, 1993.

_____. *On Virginity* in NPNF² 5.

_____. *The Great Catechism* in NPNF² 5.

Gregory Palamas. *Homilies*. 10, 11, 31 and 53 in *Saint Gregory Palamas: The Homilies*, C. Veniamin, trans. Dalton, PA: Mount Thabor Publishing, 2009.

_____. *A New Testament Decalogue* in *The Philokalia*, vol. 4, G. E. H. Palmer, Philip Sherrard & Kallistos Ware, trans. London: Faber and Faber, 1995.

_____. *Prosopopoeia* in PG 150: 960–988.

_____. *Topics of Natural and Philosophical Science and on the Moral and Ascetic Life* in *The Philokalia*, vol. 4.

_____. *To the Most Reverend Nun Xenia* in *The Philokalia*, vol. 4.

_____. *The Triads*, N. Gendle, trans. Mahwah, NJ: Paulist Press, 1983. Note: This volume does not contain the complete text. For items that it does not include, see *Défense des saints hésychastes*, 2 vols. J. Meyendorff, ed. and trans. Louvain: Peeters, 1959.

Gregory of Sinai. *On Stillness* in *The Philokalia*, vol. 4.

Hermas. *The Shepherd of Hermas* in ANF 2.

Irenaeus of Lyons. *Against the Heresies* in ANF 1.

_____. *On the Apostolic Preaching*, John Behr, trans. Popular Patristics Series, vol. 17. Crestwood, NY: St Vladimir's Seminary Press, 1997.

Isaac the Syrian. *Ascetical Homilies*. The author refers to the numbering of the French translation, which is based on the Greek text: *Discours ascétiques* in *Isaac le Syrien: Œuvres spirituelles*, J. Touraille trans. Paris: Desclée de Brouwer, 1981. In English: *The Ascetical Homilies of Saint Isaac the Syrian*. Translated by Holy

Transfiguration Monastery. 2nd ed. Boston, MA: Holy Transfiguration Monastery, 2011.

John Cassian. *The Conferences* in NPNF² 11 or *John Cassian: The Conferences*. Boniface Ramsey, trans. New York, Paulist Press, 1997.

_____. *The Institutes* in NPNF² or *John Cassian: The Institutes*, B. Ramsay, trans. New York: The Newman Press, 2000.

John Chrystostom. *Commentary on the Psalms* in *St John Chrysostom: Commentary on the Psalms*, 2 vols. R. C. Hill, trans. Brookline, MA: Holy Cross Orthodox Press, 1998.

_____. *Homily on the Consolation of Death*. In French: *Homélie sur la consolation de la mort*, available along with his *Œuvres complètes* at *www.abbaye-saint-benoit.ch/saints/chrysostome*.

_____. *Homily on the Resurrection of the Dead*. In French: *Homélie sur la résurrection des morts* in *Homélies sur la Résurrection, l'Ascension et la Pentcôte*, vol.1, N. Rambault, trans. Paris: Éditions du Cerf, 2013.

_____. *Six Homilies on Isaiah 6*. In *St. John Chrysostom: Old Testament Homilies, Volume Two: Homilies on Isaiah and Jeremiah*. Robert Charles Hill, trans. Brookline, MA: Holy Cross Orthodox Press, 2003. pp. 41–113.

_____. *Homilies on 1 Thessalonians* in NPNF¹ 13.

_____. *Homilies on Genesis* in *St John Chrysostom: Homilies on Genesis 1–67*, 3 vols., R. C. Hill, trans. Washington, DC: Catholic University of America Press, 1985–92.

_____. *Homilies on the Gospel of St John* in NPNF¹ 14.

_____. *Homilies on the Gospel of St Matthew* in NPNF¹ 10.

_____. *Homilies on Philippians* in NPNF¹ 13.

_____. *Homilies on the Statues* in NPNF¹ 9.

_____. *Homilies on 1 and 2 Corinthians* in NPNF¹ 12.

_____. *First Homily on Marriage* in *Homélies sur le mariage*, available at *www.abbaye-saint-benoit.ch/saints/chrysostome*.

_____. *Three Homilies Concerning the Power of Demons* in NPNF¹ 9.

_____. *On Choosing a Wife* in *On Marriage and Family Life*, C. P. Roth and D. Anderson, trans. Popular Patristics Series, vol. 7. Crestwood, NY: St Vladimir's Seminary Press, 1987.

_____. *On Virginity* in *On Virginity, Against Remarriage*, Sally Rieger Shore, trans. NY: E. Mellen Press, 1983.

John Climacus. *The Ladder of Divine Ascent*, C. Luibheid & N. Russell, trans. New York: Paulist Press, 1982.

John of Damascus. *An Exact Exposition of the Orthodox Faith* in NPNF^2 9.

_____. *Sacred Parallels*. PG 95:1070–1588.

John of Gaza. *Letters* in *Barsanuphius and John: Letters*, Volume 1, John Chryssavgis, trans. Washington, DC: CUA Press, 2006. See also *Letters from the Desert: Barsanuphius and John, a Selection of Questions and Responses*. John Chryssavgis, trans. and ed. Popular Patristics Series, vol. 26. Crestwood, NY: St Vladimir's Seminary Press, 2003.

Justin Martyr. *On the Resurrection* in ANF 1.

Macarius of Egypt. *Letter to His Spiritual Sons* in Tim Vivian, *Words to Live By*, Kalamazoo, MI: Cistercian Publications, 2005.

_____. *Paraphrase of the Homilies* by St Symeon Metaphrastis in *The Philokalia*, vol. 3, G.E.H.Palmer, Philip Sherrard & Kallistos Ware, trans. London: Faber and Faber, 1984.

_____. *Pseudo-Macarius: The Fifty Spiritual Homilies and the Great Letter*, George A. Maloney, trans. New York and Mahwah, NJ: Paulist Press, 1992.

Mark the Monk. *On the Incarnation* in *Counsels on the Spiritual Life*, T. Vivian and A. Cassiday, trans. Popular Patristics Series, vol. 37. Crestwood, NY: St Vladimir's Seminary Press, 2009.

Maximus the Confessor. *Ambigua*. 7 and 42 in *On the Cosmic Mystery of Jesus Christ: Selected Writings from St Maximus the Confessor*, P. M. Blowers and R. L. Wilken, trans. Popular Patristics Series, vol. 25. Crestwood, NY: St Vladimir's Seminary Press, 2003. These—together with *Ambigua* 10, 20, 41, 43 and 45—are also available in English in *On Difficulties in the Church Fathers: The*

Ambigua, 2 vols. N. Constas, trans. Cambridge, MA: Harvard University Press, 2014.

_____. *Centuries on Love* in *The Philokalia*, vol. 2, G. E. H. Palmer, Philip Sherrard & Kallistos Ware, trans. London: Faber and Faber, 1981.

_____. *Letters* in *Saint Maxime le Confesseur: Lettres*, E. Ponsoye trans. Paris: Éditions du Cerf, 1998.

_____. *Mystagogia = The Church's Mystagogy* in *Maximus the Confessor: Selected Works*, G. C. Berthold, trans. New York: Paulist Press, 1985.

_____. *On the Lord's Prayer* in *The Philokalia*, vol. 2.

_____. *Opuscules*. 7 in A. Louth, *Maximus the Confessor*, London and New York: Routledge, 1996. 8, 9 in *Maxime le Confesseur: Opuscules théologiques et polémiques*, E. Ponsoye, trans. Paris: Éditions du Cerf, 1998.

_____. *Questions and Doubts*, Despina D. Prassas, trans. DeKalb, Ill: Northern Illinois University Press, 2010.

_____. *Questions to Thalassius*. 6, 21, 42, 61 in *On the Cosmic Mystery of Jesus Christ: Selected Writings from St Maximus the Confessor*, P. M. Blowers and R. L. Wilken, trans. Popular Patristics Series, vol. 25. Crestwood, NY: St Vladimir's Seminary Press, 2003. Introduction, 3, 25, 33, 40, 41, 50, 51, 59, 65, in *Questions à Thalassios*, 2 vols. F. Vinel, trans. Paris: Éditions du Cerf, 1992. Vol.1 2010, vol.2, 2012.

_____. *Various Texts on Theology, the Divine Economy, and Virtue and Vice* in *The Philokalia*, vol. 2.

Methodius of Olympus. *The Banquet of the Ten Virgins* in ANF 6.

Nemesius of Emesa. *On the Nature of Man* in PG 40:504–18.

Nicetas Stethatos. *On the Inner Nature of Things and on the Purification of the Intellect* in *The Philokalia*, vol. 4.

_____. *On the Soul* (*De l'âme*) in *Nicétas Stéthatos: Opuscules et lettres*, J. Darrouzès, trans. and ed. Sources Chrétiennes 81. Paris: Éditions du Cerf, 1961.

_____. *On Spiritual Knowledge, Love and the Perfection of Living* in *The Philokalia*, vol. 4.

_____. *Letters* in J. Darrouzès.

Nicodemus of the Holy Mountain. *A Handbook of Spiritual Counsels*, P. A. Chamberas, trans. New York: Paulist Press, 1989.

Nicephorus the Monk. *On Watchfulness and the Guarding of the Heart* in *The Philokalia*, vol. 4.

Origen. *Fragments on Romans* refers to the Greek fragments in Jean Scherer, *Le commentaire d'Origéne sur Rom. III.5–V.7 d'aprés les extraits du Papyrus no. 88748 du Musée du Caire et les fragments de la Philocalie et du Vaticanus Gr.762: Essai de reconstitution du texte et de la pensée des tomes V et VI du "Commentaire sur l'Épître aux Romains."* Le Caire: Institut français d'archéologie orientale, 1957.

Philo of Alexandria. *On the Creation* in *The Works of Philo Judaeus*, C. D. Yonge, trans. London, H. G. Bohn, 1854–1890. Available at *www.earlychristianwritings.com/yonge*.

Serapion of Thmuis. *Letter to the Monks* in *Sarapion of Thmuis: Against the Manicheans and Pastoral Letters*. Oliver Herbel, trans. Sydney, NSW: St Paul's Publications, 2011.

Symeon Metaphrastis. *Paraphrase of the Homilies of St Macarius of Egypt* in *The Philokalia*, vol. 3.

Symeon the New Theologian. *The Practical and Theological Chapters and the Three Theological Discourses*, P. McGuckin, trans. Kalamazoo, MI: Cistercian Publications, 1982.

_____. *The Ethical Discourses* in *Symeon the New Theologian: On the Mystical Life. The Ethical Discourses*, vol. 2. Alexander Golitzin, trans. Popular Patristics Series, vol. 15. Crestwood, NY: St Vladimir's Seminary Press, 1996.

_____. *The Three Methods of Prayer* in *The Philokalia*, vol. 4.

Tertullian. *On the Resurrection* in ANF 3.

Theodoret of Cyrus. *On Divine Providence* in *Theodoret of Cyrus: On Divine Providence*, Thomas Halton, trans. Mahwah, NJ: Paulist Press, 1988.

_____. *Commentary on Romans* in *Theodoret of Cyrus: Commentary on the Letters of St Paul*, vol.1, Robert C. Hill, trans. Brookline, MA: Holy Cross Orthodox Press, 2001.

Theodoros the Great Ascetic. *A Century of Spiritual Texts* in *The Philokalia*, vol. 2.

Theoliptos of Philadelphia. *On Inner Work in Christ and the Monastic Profession* in *ThePhilokalia*, vol. 4.

_____. *Texts* in *The Philokalia*, vol. 4.

Theophilus of Antioch. *To Autolycus* in ANF 2.